The History of Civilization

Edited by C K. OGDEN, M.A.

CHINA AND EUROPE

Intellectual and Artistic Contacts in the
Eighteenth Century

China and Europe

Intellectual and Artistic Contacts in the Eighteenth Century

By

ADOLF   REICHWEIN

LONDON
ROUTLEDGE & KEGAN PAUL LTD

First published in Great Britain 1925
by Kegan Paul, Trench, Trubner & Co. Ltd

Reissued 1968

by Routledge & Kegan Paul Ltd
Broadway House, 68–74 Carter Lane
London, E.C.4

Printed in Great Britain
by Lowe & Brydone (Printers) Ltd, London

TRANSLATED BY
J. C. POWELL

SBN 7100 4975 7

CONTENTS

PAGE

INTRODUCTION: THE YOUNGER GENERATION OF TO-DAY AND THE
WISDOM OF THE EAST 1

The threefold bridge to Lao Tzŭ and his doctrine: inward
orientation of life—Wu-wei and non-action (Lao Tzŭ-Tolstoi)
—Return to Nature (Lao Tzŭ-Rousseau-Tolstoi).

BRIEF REVIEW OF THE CONTACTS BETWEEN EUROPE AND CHINA
UP TO THE END OF THE EIGHTEENTH CENTURY . . 13

The economic contacts—Literature on China—Opinions of
the East.

ROCOCO 23

Feeling of style in the Rococo—Affinity of feeling between
Rococo and ancient Chinese culture—Porcelain: importation
and influence on the style of European ornament—Invention
of European porcelain—Lacquer: importance of Chinese and
Japanese lacquer for the development of European furniture-
style—European lacquer—Its applications—Silk: importation
of silk—Its importance for the development of European
weaving and of European ornament—Chinese embroideries in
Europe—Their influence on the European technique—
Naturalization of Chinese wall-papers in Europe—Painting:
"chinoiserie," especially in Watteau, Pillement—Architecture:
adoption of Chinese motives—Imitations of Chinese temples,
pleasure-houses, pagodas—European-Chinese mixed style:
Pillnitz and the Summer Palace of Peking—Change in treatment of interiors under Chinese influence—" Chinoiseries " in
social and public life—China and the stage—Comedy, music-
drama—Satire and " Lettres chinoises."

THE ENLIGHTENMENT 73

Character of the enlightenment period—Its contact with
China by way of Confucius—The admirers of China: Leibniz,
Wolff, Voltaire and the Encyclopædists—The sceptics:
Frederick the Great, Montesquieu—The opponents: Rousseau,
Fénelon.

THE PHYSIOCRATS 99

Derivation of Quesnay's physiocratic theory of political
economy from the ancient Chinese doctrine of the State
and its relation to Society.

THE AGE OF FEELING 111

Origin of " Feeling "—England—Its art: in the garden—
Adoption of the Chinese style of garden—The English-Chinese
garden—Its diffusion over Europe—Development of water-
colour painting under Chinese influence.

v

CONTENTS

PAGE

GOETHE 127

Fin de siècle—Distaste—Ripeness of judgment on the East—
Apartness—Subjective dislike for imperfectly represented
Chinese art—Objective value of Chinese culture in the world
of Goethe as an old man—Goethe and literature on China—
Chinese influences: Elpenor, Chinesisch-deutsche Jahres-
und Tageszeiten—Note on the criticism of sources—Interpretation.

LAST WORDS 147

Dying out of the enthusiasm for the Far East in the agitated
close of the eighteenth century—Revival of the European
antique—Rise of the Indian world.

NOTES 155

INDEX 169

LIST OF ILLUSTRATIONS
PLATES
(at the end of book)

FIGURE

1. KANG-HSI VASE
2. EIGHTEENTH-CENTURY TEAPOT WITH CHINESE FIGURES
3. EIGHTEENTH-CENTURY LACQUERED FRENCH COMMODE
4. CHINESE WOVEN SILK TAPESTRY
5. CHINESE PAINTING ON SILK
6. CHINESE FAN, PAINTED, WITH LACQUERED SPOKES
7. CHINOISERIE OF WATTEAU
8. FROM PILLEMENT'S SERIES OF PRINTS
9. FRENCH ENGRAVING OF CHINESE BATTLE SCENE
10. FRENCH ENGRAVING OF CHINESE BATTLE SCENE
11. MUNICH, THE QUEEN'S SALON
12. THE 'JAPANISCHER PAVILLON' AT SANS-SOUCI
13. THE CHINESE INFLUENCE ON FURNITURE
14. IMITATION OF LATTICE WORK
15. FRENCH COMMODE, EIGHTEENTH CENTURY
16. SOWING RICE
17. CHINESE RICE FARMERS
18. DOORWAY AT CLAYDON HOUSE
19. 'CHINESE' BEDROOM AT CLAYDON HOUSE
20. PAGODA IN SHANGHAI
21. PAGODA IN KEW GARDENS
24. PO YO BRIDGE
25. THE GARDEN AT STOURHEAD, WILTS.
26. LACQUERED CABINET AT CHARLOTTENBURG

ILLUSTRATIONS IN THE TEXT

	page
22. HEADPIECE	113
23. PLAN FOR THE ANGLO-CHINESE GARDEN OF THE PETIT TRIANON	117

vii

INTRODUCTION

THE YOUNGER GENERATION OF TO-DAY AND THE WISDOM OF THE EAST

INTRODUCTION

" WE Europeans are beginning to be educated by ancient China ": thus did Alphonse Paquet some ten years ago summarize the feeling of a small group of cosmopolitan thinkers and students of the East. The writings of the Chinese sages form for many of the younger generation of our day a necessary link in the chain of their intellectual experiences, for many others unfortunately merely a part of that world-literature which they treat as a storehouse of literary delicacies. Western and Eastern culture are by such persons frequently shuffled together with a sometimes amazing lack of precision —an example of the prevalence of slovenly thinking, that ' synthetic ' thinking of which there is so much talk nowadays.

But even this conversational ' mode ' is only the distorted reflection of a real inner relation. Rudolf Eucken spoke recently of the " immeasurable importance of a closer connexion between East and West," and already during the War Nathorp made the following forecast: " To-day," he said, " the expiring occidental turns his face back to the rising-place of the spiritual sun, the true birthplace of Man and of all his profound dreams of God and the Soul—to the East."

The East proudly echoed his words. Tagore spoke: " For if this brand consume itself and be extinguished, leaving a heap of ashes as its only memorial, the everlasting light will once more shine forth in the East—in the East where human history had its dawn." And Ku Hung-ming, not a lyric poet like Tagore, but a commonsense Confucian, gives Europe the practical advice to learn at last from China " the religion of the good citizen," and so recover from its malady of division between ' Power-worship ' and ' Mob-worship.'

Even to the casual observer it cannot but be obvious to-day that forces are here at work which have long since passed beyond the narrow circle of the *dilettanti* and, in ways most various and difficult to trace, have taken hold of a wider public, which includes all the troubled and agitated spirits of our age. Whether this ' Asiatic fever ' is merely destined to reveal to the West its own decadence and to lead it back to *its own sources*, or whether we have here the real beginning of a great transformation in the entire spiritual adjustment of the Western world, the coming century will decide.

Eastern Asia has in any case for the second time in European history—the first was when the eighteenth century declared its intellectual affinity with that world—entered into metaphysical contact with the West.

Especially upon that section of the younger generation which is disturbed by the spiritual problems of the age has the secure tranquillity of Oriental wisdom made a lasting impression. Opinions may differ as to whether this makes for good or for evil: we will not concern ourselves here with that question, but only with the spiritual condition which has created for itself such organs of understanding. It must be said here that the younger generation of to-day is only a particularly sensitive index of that which agitates the age generally. It has no right to separate itself from that age, is indeed more deeply rooted in it than others, more richly dowered, perhaps, than any age for a long time past, and for that reason under obligation to adopt an attitude of humility and responsibility towards the past. Youth—the season of the opening blossom, of the vivid blood—has always been more alive to what is ' in the air,' and therefore cannot help giving to these sensations more definite and positive expression than a mature and practical judgment can always approve. We should, therefore, not be in too great a hurry to ridicule its Oriental leanings, but rather endeavour to fix our attention on the religious impulse which underlies this attitude.

In *A Message to Asia*—full of youthful fervour and exuberance—we read the words, " Demonstrate to Earth that it can be dominated by no other culture than that of the soul." Here we have in its most acute expression that which is on its way as the antithesis to the nineteenth century — the endeavour to give an inward direction to life.

To this often eschatological yearning for an inward development, which, especially after the shocks and upheavals of the last decade, has made its appearance in numbers of small groups, Lao Tzŭ came as a great luminary. The *Tao Tē Ching* became for the present generation a bridge between

East and West. Since the opening of the present century
no less than eight translations of it have appeared in
Germany. It is a little surprising in this connexion to notice
the irritation displayed by various Chinese scholars, who can
see nothing but the philological shortcomings of these translations: Otto Franck, for instance, speaking of the *Tao Tē
Ching* in the *Archiv für Religionswissenschaft* (xiii, 130),
condemns the translation-mania, while an English scholar
cannot understand how it is that the *Tao Tē Ching* has
exercised such an uninterrupted attraction not only on
students of Chinese but on others as well. The translations,
which are certainly not all made from the originals, are
significant mainly as present-day confessions of faith, in the
name of ' The Old Man of the East,' and not as philological
masterpieces.

In Lao Tzŭ the *Tao* denotes " emptiness and tranquillity ";
the devout Taoist listens for the whisperings of his innermost
self, which is also the heart of the world. One who, after all
the noise and rush of a mechanical age, needs quiet and
retirement, learns from Lao Tzŭ to overcome the outer world
in the *Tao*. The demand of our time for inwardness of life
finds an answer here.

And this very withdrawal into the innermost and most
tranquil region of the soul naturally produces that ' passive '
frame of mind, which we so often meet with to-day. Not in
the sense of *dolce far niente*, but of something much more
strenuous. Everywhere nowadays we find young men to
whom the *Wu-wei* of Lao Tzŭ has come as a revelation, and
the best of them belong decidedly to the effective, conquering
type of manhood. And here the influence of those two great
teachers Lao Tzŭ and Tolstoi unites in one current. And,
for the man who owes allegiance to both, their ethic of ' in-
action ' becomes a duty. Tolstoi knew that in this central
article of his teaching he was at one with Lao Tzŭ, and he
even planned a Russian translation of the *Tao Tē Ching*.
He owns that for him the saying of the Sermon on the Mount:
" But I say unto you that you shall not resist the evil,"
contained the key to all wisdom. And from Lao Tzŭ, who
was equally certain of the cosmic solution of the opposition
between good and evil, we have the saying: " Between Yea
and Nay what difference is there ? Between Good and Evil

what difference is there ?" Here we have the root of the negative Anarchism which unites Tolstoi and Lao Tzŭ.

The demand for a sedative to meet the restlessness of the times has, of course, its deep significance; but for youth with its natural tendency to excess it contains a danger. When Lao Tzŭ is accepted as such a sedative, there easily follows that general dislike and dread of action which is so often found in the youthful movements of the day, opposed as a negative to the positive ' Activism ' of the age. And Stählin (*Fieber und Heil in der Jugendbewegung*) rightly sees in both a particular kind of barren flight from life. To many who are inclined to confuse their own lack of clearness and keenness with the pure mysticism of Lao Tzŭ, Stählin's reproach would undoubtedly apply: " Voices from the near and the far East," he says, have " brought to some of you your first impressions of that Wisdom which our Western omniscience lacks, but, unless you combine this insight with the rigorous thinking of the West, you must not be surprised if all your enthusiasm about the mysticism and the wisdom of the East is set down as mere lack of intellectual discipline." One would like to remind these people of Goethe's saying: " Only by active work on very definite and strictly limited tasks can higher culture be attained." The *Wu-wei*, the principle of abstention from action, may have inspired in a few a certain nobility of mental attitude, but for the majority of those who in our time have been captivated by it, it has been a distorting mirror.

The cry of ' Back to Nature ' forms a third link between certain of the younger generation and the ancient wisdom of the *Tao Tē Ching*.

The feeling of the Fall of Man involved in the mechanization of our age is widely spread, and many attempts have been made to escape from the toils. The efforts of man to liberate himself from the unfelt restraint of the natural cycles is regarded as the last stage in a process of decadence, culminating in the destruction of all cohesion in the mass-individualism of our time. Here also, as in almost all questions relating to the crises of civilization, we have two parties—on one side, the champions of progress, who, in spite of all the stresses and strains of the age, see in the growth of technique a great step in advance towards a brilliant future; on the other, a

number of people whose minds are in various degrees steeped
in romantic feelings more or less of the Rousseau type. For
these latter Lao Tzŭ is one of the prophets of the Life according to Nature: they have lost that belief in the unimpeded
progress of human culture and ethical improvement which
was characteristic of the nineteenth century—they would
like to restore primitive conditions. Return to 'Harmony
with Nature' was one of the catchwords of the '*Jeunesse*'
movement; it is the same tendency which encourages the
spread of 'Eurhythmics,' which demands the unhampered
development of the creative powers even in the child—everywhere we have the effort to get back into the natural cycles.
Such was the doctrine of Lao Tzŭ, who sought to bring the
human *Tao* into harmony with the *Tao* of the cosmos. It is
the same sceptical attitude towards the institutions of customary right, of morality, of civilization generally, which
links Lao Tzŭ with Rousseau and again with Tolstoi, and
which appeals so strongly to the young man of to-day. It is
that attitude of mind which feels as decadence what others
call progress; whereby is understood the transition from
natural activity prompted by love and common interests, and
from the spontaneous activity of the natural man to the
legally regulated life of modern civilization, in which the
civic morality of the organized state prevails. Lao Tzŭ had
recognized in his time the inner falsity which was eating out
the soul of his people, how they made great play with ideals
which had no longer any meaning for them, but only survived
as words. He saw that the only remedy lay in deep con-
templation, in forgetting all the fine formulæ which had so
little reality, in listening to the voice of man's innermost
being—which was one with the universal Being.

He looked upon the work of Kung Fu-tzŭ as an attempt with
inadequate means, a mere treatment of the symptoms, when
what was wanted was a radical cure. "The great Reason,"
he says, "was deserted; thus came Morality and Duty.
Cleverness and Knowledge arose: thus came the great lies.
Among men of one blood divisions arose: so came Duty to
Parents and Love of Parents. The state fell into strife and
confusion: so came loyal servants." (*Tao Tē Ching*, Saying
18.) Or in another place: "Does Life fail, then Love. Does
Love fail, then Justice. Does Justice fail, then Morality.

This Morality is lack of Truth and Faith and the beginning of confusion." (Saying 38.) Even more caustically and with Rousseau-like ruthlessness he says: " Give up Art, have done with gain, and there will be no more thieves and robbers." (Saying 19.) One is reminded of Rousseau's answer to the prize-question of the Dijon Academy, whether Science and Art tended to the improvement of mankind. And Tolstoi, who had been familiar with Rousseau from his fifteenth year, who hated music because it intoxicated men and robbed them of their calm reason and of their accord with Nature, has brought back into our age this spirit of absorption in Nature. It is interesting to notice in this connexion that in Lao Tzŭ are to be found the words: "Music and Sweetmeats, they cause the traveller to halt by the way. The *Tao* goes forth from the mouth mild and without flavour. You look for it and see nothing remarkable. You listen for it and hear nothing remarkable; you act on it and never come to an end." (Saying 35.)

Seventy years ago, Tolstoi ridiculed the belief in progress as a " strange religion of his times," and, like Lao Tzŭ (since each felt his world crumble in his grasp, leaving behind only the baseless particulars), he found his only salvation in that saving of the Soul which he held that every man must set about by getting into touch with the pure essence of his own Being. " Man's task in life is to save his Soul. That he may save his Soul, Man must live like God; and that he may live like God, he must forsake all the pleasures of Life "; and Lao Tzŭ had said the same thing in like words: "So that the Holy man takes thought for that which is within and takes no thought for the delights of the eye." (Saying 12.) Thus, for Lao Tzŭ and Tolstoi and for all who can accept their teaching, Differentiation returns to Identity, and that which the arbitrary activity of thought had broken up into a confused multiplicity is thereby brought back to the simplicity of original Nature. This ' Return to Nature ' is often accompanied by a leaning to pantheism, which likewise appears in various forms in the present day. It is remarkable that Lao Tzŭ, in opposition to Kung Fu-tzŭ, conceived the *Tao* as cosmic—as having come into being before the Lord of Heaven himself and as permeating all things. " The *Tao* works in ways we cannot perceive nor understand. Invisible and incomprehensible, yet within it things are! Unfathomable and dark, yet within it is seed! The seed is the truth. In the truth is faith." (Saying 21.)

Some have seen here—Rudolf Pannwitz, for instance—the possibility, not indeed of an ideal religiosity devoid of positive content, which is not what they are seeking, but of a world-religion—a ' summa religionum mundi '—to which the various religions might form a preparation. Pannwitz seeks in this way to give a positive direction to our despairing relativism. " An overwhelming thought!" he says, " that at the moment when all our traditions have broken down and we find ourselves cast, like shipwrecked mariners, solitary on the most dismal of shores, at that very moment the whole many-coloured, creative past of mankind is presented to us as our buried treasure, our Troy to be excavated, and the horizon of our future is enlarged almost *ad infinitum.*" And further: " In Nietzsche lies, for him who has eyes to see, a religion of the future—a complete and perfect religion. It is akin to the religion of the ancient East—once more a religion of the whole Cosmos." (Pannwitz, *Weltreligion :* in *Geisteskultur und Volksbildung* [" Monatshefte der Comenius-Gesellschaft," July-August, 1921, pp. 155-6].)

This is unmeasured language. It could only have come from the restless extravagance of a mind which, having lost its historical moorings, has formed utterly perverse notions of its own time and the good which it contains. And yet measure is more than ever necessary in our time. Indeed, I think that those who accept as a revelation the wonderful and profound mysticism of Lao Tzŭ would do well to remember that saying of his: " The wider your range, the less your knowledge." (Saying 47.)

That the East has been an inspiration to our younger generation we would not and cannot deny; but only if this plunge into another world, which is at bottom an effect of our own crisis, should lead to a recovered knowledge of ourselves, only then could we see in it an event of deep significance. Only then should we rid ourselves of a form of thought with which the younger generation is fond of disguising the tentative character of its own thinking-paradox. The question needs investigation—how it comes about that paradox becomes more effective and therefore more important precisely at those moments when dying cultures, in so far as they contain within them the germs of future development, reach breaking-point. Here we would only point out that Lao Tzŭ, placed as he was at a similar turning-point, was likewise fond of that suggestive but ambiguous figure. One of his short sayings reveals the secret of his method— " True words are as it were inverted." (Saying 78.)

For the sake of exactness it should not be forgotten that, even if Lao Tzŭ be supreme in the hearts of those who to-day make a cult of Orientalism, Kung Fu-tzŭ has not altogether been discredited as a teacher. On the contrary he is frequently cited by those whose interest lies not so much in the intellectual problems of their age as in working out on commonsense lines sound and plain principles of citizenship. In their eyes, Lao Tzŭ's mysticism is the work of a perhaps profound but quite unpractical enthusiast, which is perhaps even in its fundamental anarchism nonsensical and not to be reconciled with human reality. It cannot be ignored that, even before the War, the writings of the strict Confucian, Ku Hung-ming, had made a deep impression in Germany; and Pannwitz, in his work on *The Crisis in European Culture*, though he is primarily concerned with theoretical problems, always comes back to his one prepossession—the ordering of society on the solid, sure and civilizing principles formulated for ancient China by Kung Fu-tzŭ. It is a significant fact also that the group of political philosophers which centres round Nelson of Göttingen should have been responsible for the publishing of a collection of Ku Hung-ming's essays in a German translation. In these essays Europe is urged, as it was two hundred years ago, to follow the example of Confucian philosophy and to get a clear insight into the " fundamental concepts " in order that Europe, like China of old, may construct for itself on that basis a solid conception of the world, and thereby attain to more stable political conditions.

If we may be allowed to make in passing a rough distinction, we should say that, of the two groups which in the present day have an intellectual interest in the East, the one was irrational, consisting of the followers of Lao Tzŭ, the other rational, consisting of those who are attracted by Kung Fu-tzŭ. In view of present-day intellectual tendencies it is only natural that the former should attract more attention.

This mainly irrational attitude of the younger generation suggests a contrast between it and the philosophical movement of the eighteenth century known as the ' Enlightenment,' of which we shall have something to say in the following pages.

We shall there describe, not in detail but in a summary sketch, the relations of the West with the East during a whole century, with the object of showing in a particular case in what various ways these intellectual relations are formed— and intellectual relations often underlie the most external and concrete—and how they are perpetually in a state of change corresponding to the changing needs of those who, owing to some lack, are in the position of recipients.

The fact that the number of those who are, for one reason or another, interested in the East is nowadays considerable, seems to justify the present work. It does not claim to contain a complete treatment of the subject. On the contrary it is intentionally limited to a compressed presentation of matters which, on the basis of the material collected, could have been treated more fully. If this has not been done, it is because the purpose of the book is merely to give a short introduction to the subject defined in our title.

BRIEF REVIEW OF THE CONTACTS BETWEEN EUROPE AND CHINA UP TO THE END OF THE EIGHTEENTH CENTURY

CONTACTS OF EUROPE WITH CHINA

OUR knowledge of the relations of the West with the Far East goes back to before the Christian era. Even before our ancestors had entered upon their struggle with the Roman Empire, the annals of the Chinese Emperors contain accounts of Roman doings.[1] During the Middle Ages communication with China by way of the interior of Asia was always maintained. Marco Polo's famous account of his travels gives us a vivid picture of these relations at the height of that period.[2] But it was the discovery of the sea passage to the East Indies that first brought about that more intimate connexion with the legendary ' Cathay ' which during the following centuries became more and more firmly established. Some·years earlier, Christopher Columbus had sailed forth in the hope of reaching the Far East and its fabulous riches. And, after his landing in America, he continued to believe that the countries which he had discovered were continuous with the Kingdom of Cathay. The island of La Juana seemed to him so vast that he took it for a province of Cathay. In his letters he expresses his delight at having found in Zepangu, *i.e.*, Cuba, much cotton-wool which he hoped to sell at a good profit in the populous cities of the Great Khan. Columbus had learnt about Cathay—China—from Marco Polo's book. His copy of it with his marginal notes is preserved in the Bibliotheca Columbina in Seville.

With the discovery of the Far East by the Portuguese, sailing in an opposite direction, the circle of the earth was practically completed. The irresistible enterprise of the discoverers of the Renaissance and Baroque periods broke through the barriers which had for ages shut off the most distant regions of the Earth.

The Portuguese having established permanent communications with the Far East, the Western world was able during the sixteenth and seventeenth centuries to gain clearer and clearer ideas of the Chinese Empire.

15

In order to make this plainer, I propose to set down here the most important facts bearing on the development of trade with the East and on the literature of the subject in the sixteenth and seventeenth centuries. For first the importations of porcelain, silk, lacquer-work, and many other precious products of the Chinese Empire aroused the attention, curiosity and admiration of the great European public, and then literature set to work to keep alive and further to stimulate these feelings. Thus trade and literature, however strange the juxtaposition may seem, co-operated in producing the frame of mind which in the first half of the eighteenth century was to secure for China so prominent a place in the fashions of Europe.

The history of trade with China since the discovery of the sea-route is in brief as follows.*

While the Portuguese, after their first landing in China in 1515, had in their hands the bulk of China trade in the sixteenth century, in the seventeenth it was the Dutch who commanded the East Asiatic market. (During the first fifty years of that century they had captured three hundred Portuguese vessels. In the eighteenth century the Dutch were displaced by the English.) The Dutch East India Company, which (after 1602 under the title of Company for Greater India) had absorbed all the earlier companies, during the period 1603–1693 imported from East India and especially from China—for the goods bought in East India came partly from China—goods to the annual value of 120 million livres. (In later years these figures were doubled and trebled.) In 1653 this one Company was able to show a profit of 51 million livres, and in 1693 of almost 100 millions.[3] These figures show with what astounding rapidity importations from China into Europe rose, in spite of the fact that in those days transport was comparatively slow, while it was only in answer to increased demand and the prospects of large profits that the hold-capacity began to be enlarged.[4] Between the years 1602 and 1730 the Dutch company distributed to its shareholders 300 million marks in dividends, or 21·17 per

* It should be noted at the outset that precise figures of European trade with China exclusively are not obtainable. As a rule, it is the totals of all East Indian imports—cargoes loaded in China, Japan, Upper and Lower India—which are given in the accounts and contracts. Nevertheless, even from these figures a fairly correct idea of the imports from China itself may be obtained.

cent. of the capital.[5]   And in spite of this it appeared in 1730 that the Company was working with a deficit of 400 million marks.[6]   It was unable in the long run to guard itself against the corruption of its own officials.   In addition to this the English, during the seventeenth century, had been surely and methodically advancing the centre of gravity of their trade from Persia to the Far East, India, and China.[7] Towards the end of the seventeenth century the English company was bringing Eastern wares into Europe to the value of 18 million marks per annum.[8]   It suffered heavy losses, it is true, through the wars with the Mogul (1680), which ended in the temporary withdrawal of the English from Bombay and Surat.   Then came the Revolution at home.   But in 1698, after the Peace of Ryswick, English trade had already recovered, and a new company was founded which, with the help of the Navigation Act of 1651, succeeded in a few decades in outstripping its Dutch rival.

A passage from Voltaire may throw light on the vast proportions which trade relations with India and China had assumed.   It was, of course, not written until the second half of the eighteenth century, but it is equally true of the sixteenth and seventeenth: " People ask," he says, " what becomes of all the gold and silver which is continually flowing into Spain from Peru and Mexico.   It goes into the pockets of Frenchmen and Englishmen and Dutchmen, who carry on trade in Cadiz, and in return send the products of their industries to America.   A large part of this money goes to the East Indies and pays for silk, spices, saltpetre, sugar-candy, tea, textiles, diamonds and curios."[9]

When we consider how enormously the amount of gold and silver in Europe had increased at this period, we obtain indirectly a rough idea of European trade with the East.

About the year 1500, the bullion supply of Europe amounted to—   Gold: 8,369,000 kg.
                  Silver: 77,000,000 kg.

Between 1493 and 1600 this figure was increased by
                  Gold: 754,000 kg.
                  Silver: 22,835,000 kg.

Between 1601 and 1700 there was a further increase of
                  Gold: 912,000 kg.
                  Silver: 37,835,000 kg.[10]

In comparison with the competition between England and Holland French trade played but a small part, in spite of the efforts of Colbert. About 1660, for example, the ocean-going shipping of Europe is estimated at about 20,000 vessels. To this total Holland contributed 1,600, while France owned no more than about 600 ships. Colbert's ship-building did indeed increase this figure, but hardly affected the position of France in relation to the other nations. The trade of the *Compagnie des Indes Orientales*, founded by Colbert, in 1664, amounted to less than three million livres per annum. By far the greater part of her Chinese imports reached France by way of Holland. But, if the part played by her in the development of trade-relations with China was insignificant, her influence as intellectual middleman between China and Europe was immense.

The development of European literature in its bearings on China can, of course, only be treated here in brief outline and from one point of view. We shall try to show how the changes in European notions about China were reflected in European literature.

Marco Polo's book had been nothing more than a geographical treatise, a mere string of experiences. The first missionary reports of the sixteenth century, though they bore witness to much proselytizing ardour, and astonished the European public with stories of miraculous conversions, had hardly anything to tell of China itself. For example, the letter printed in Dillingen in 1589 and dated " from the most glorious and right royal isle of Japon and then straight from the uttermost end of the Earth, to wit from the most mighty empire of the Chinas," hardly ever refers to conditions in these countries and that only when the writer is reminded by something of his native place. For example, of the town of Cinquion it is said: " To this town which, as Père Rogerius says, very much resembles Venice ";[11] or, " In all Portugal there is no town to be compared with this, Lisbon alone excepted ";[12] or again, " Passed through a town in which the Pozzotan ware is made, that is sold all over India."[13] That is all that is said of China in the whole book. The most extraordinary stories were circulated about this mysterious Pozzotan ware, concerning which there was great curiosity at the time. It was said, for instance, that it had to remain

buried in the earth for a hundred years in order to acquire
its proper hardness, and that accordingly the artist could never
behold his own work in its full beauty.[14]   Not only porcelain, but tea also, was surrounded with a halo of legend.   The
whole country was to that age so singular and strange that
even in the seventeenth century the most incredible tales
were believed.

But these first letters of the missionaries were soon followed
by other publications, the earliest from secular sources, which
really gave some information about China.   The written
word was here helped out by pictures.   In 1596 and 1598
appeared in Holland, which at that time was already in close
touch with the East, the first Chinese portraits.   (It was
from Holland moreover that, in the second half of the seventeenth century, the French engravers of Chinese originals were
influenced.)   Soon the pictures began to be accompanied by
written explanations, and presently the ' letter press ' claimed
more space; there appeared the first illustrated reports of
embassies—the earliest, of course, being published in Holland.
Of great influence were the illustrated descriptions of the
Dutch embassies, which appeared in the years 1665–1675;
especially those by P. de Geyer and J. de Kayser (1665),
" embellished with more than 150 drawings taken from the
life in China."   The pictures were similar to the later Chinese
engravings of Jollain in France: representations of pagodas
and temples, which, as the perspective showed, were made
after Chinese originals.   It was from these Dutch plates
that the French engravers, whose works were sold in such
numbers at the fairs in the time of Louis XIV, undoubtedly
borrowed.[15]

Besides these Dutch books of travel the *Novus Atlas Sinensis
de Martino Martini* had a wide circulation.   It appeared at
Vienna in 1655 just in time to influence the work of Athanasius Kircher, then just commenced, which for decades was
the favourite authority of the lovers of things Chinese.[16]
This book, which was first published in Latin under the title
China monumentis qua sacris qua profanis illustrata, was soon
translated into French, and in 1672 a Latin edition appeared
in Berlin with music and ' corrections ' by Andreas Müller.[17]

Though Kircher's book mainly consisted of pictures, there
was a new note of scientific seriousness in his work.   This

more serious content was soon lost sight of, it is true—the
pictures made the book the China Encyclopædia of the
seventeenth century; but the work continued to exercise
influence for a long time.   It is a curious fact that almost all
through the seventeenth century, while Chinese curios filled
an important place at all the fairs, and while there was already
a widely circulated popular literature on the subject, the
learned world was not yet familiar with the new phenome-
non.   Pascal, for example, for all his erudition, died in 1662
without having acquired any particular knowledge about
China.   In his *Pensées* there is only one passage implying
any knowledge, and that passage sufficiently proves that he
knew nothing.[18]

Contemporarily with Kircher's book the first translations
of Chinese classics were placed on the European market by
the Jesuit missionaries.   In 1662 appeared in China, published
by Père Prosper Intorcetta, with woodcuts obviously in
Chinese style, Père Ignatius da Costa's translation of *The
Great Doctrine* (*Ta-hsüeh*) under the title *Sapientia Sinica*.
In 1673, Intorcetta published a translation of his own of the
Chung-yung—Intorcetta latinized the title as *Chum-yum*—
one of the four Chinese classics besides the ' 5 Ching.'   An
appendix contained a life of Confucius in Latin and French.
The general title *Sinarum scientia politicomoralis* already points
to a line of study which has been followed with ever-increasing
thoroughness by the serious literature of later times.*

In 1687 appeared the first translation of Confucius, after
that Père Philippe Couplet, in the course of his journey
through Europe, had directed attention to da Costa's *Confucius*.[19]   Here we have, struck together for the first time,
the three notes which in the learned world of the eighteenth
century were never heard apart: China—Confucius—political
morality.   Confucius is treated in this work with great
reverence; the Jesuit Father calls him ' *Sapientissimus et
moralis philosophiæ pariter ac politicæ magister et oraculum* '
(' Master and oracle most learned alike in moral and in
political philosophy ').

* There appeared, *e.g.*, in Nürnberg, in 1688, an *East- and West-
Indian and likewise Chinese Pleasure- and State-garden* and, in 1760,
Erasmus Franciscus' *Newly-polished Mirror, displaying the History,
Art, and Manners of foreign peoples, to wit the Chinese, the Japanese,
the Hindustanis and Abyssinians.*

With this last group of works, the first place as purveyors of information about China passes to the Jesuits. In a work of Père Le Comte, *China of To-day* (1699), the essence of the Oriental lore so far acquired by the missionaries is given in a single sentence: " The Siamese," he says, " whose physiognomy is familiar to Frenchmen, and who of all those Indians* have souls exactly corresponding to their bodies, are wont to say that, when Heaven distributed the gifts of Nature, it gave to the French valour and the science of war, to the Dutch shrewdness in trade, to the English the art of navigation, to the Chinese skill in government, but to themselves, the Siamese, wisdom and understanding."[20] In another passage the careful and conscientious scholar Le Comte passes a crushing judgment on the widely read reports of the traders about the East: " In this matter also it happens that travellers often deceive us because they have first been themselves deceived. How many there are who, when they come into a new country, imagine that they can learn in an instant everything that they wish to know ! Scarcely are they landed on the shore when they start to run to and fro like hungry folk, snatching greedily at every morsel that falls in their way, and fill up their journals with common reports and the idle talk of the vulgar."

The European traders perceived how such judgments might injure their credit, and lost no time in making reprisals. In 1682, a merchant, named Roques, warned the Directors of the *Compagnie des Indes Orientales* against the ambition and the ' esprit envahissant' of the Siamese missionaries.[21] And the Protestant Dutch, who since 1650 fancied themselves to be ' kings ' of the East Asiatic trade, alleged that the Jesuits had intrigued against them at the Chinese court† and were alone to blame for the fact " that their often repeated requests for free and unrestricted trade in China had been refused."[22]

As in what follows we shall hardly have occasion to touch again on this conflict of opinion, it will be well to note at once

* It was usual to give this name to all inhabitants of West and East India, and of China also.

† One is tempted to assume that, in the conflict between the Jesuitical and the commercial view of China, religion must have played an important part. Nearly all the trade of China was in the hands of the Protestant nations—the Dutch and the English. The trade of France, the only representative of Catholicism in the Far East, was insignificant. But the missionaries were mostly Frenchmen.

that up to 1760 the Jesuitical, *i.e.*, the bevevolent, view of the Chinese, as against the commercial, was the dominant view. It was only when, towards the end of the eighteenth century, considerations of economic policy came to colour all relations with China, that the commercial view gained the upper hand, and contributed largely to the growing dislike of China. On this subject we possess a remarkable piece of evidence, which probably dates from the closing years of the century: "Monsieur Sommerat is, moreover, not the only person who entirely distrusts the reports of the missionaries, although they, having long sojourned in those regions, may be presumed to have a better acquaintance with the manners, laws, and usages of the people. For some time past it has been the fashion to prefer to their evidence that even of travellers who have never journeyed through the country, who have only seen its borders, and have only been able to communicate with the natives by the aid of signs and interpreters."[23]

At the beginning of the eighteenth century, however, feelings towards the Far East were completely in accord with the reports of the missionaries. There is a certain symbolical significance in the fact that the first New Year's Day of the century was celebrated at the French court with Chinese festivities. The Rococo was at the door.

ROCOCO

ROCOCO

A RELAXATION of style is characteristic of the Rococo. The restraint of the Louis XIV period having degenerated into rigidity in all forms of life, the death of the king was inevitably followed by the licence of the Regency. The straitjacket in which thought, plastic creation, and human conduct generally had been confined, was burst asunder. The reaction which followed took the form of the Bizarre.

In the domain of philosophic thought Pierre Bayle is the most typical representative of this transitional phase of the European mind. With full consciousness he made it his task to propound problems, to point out breaks, strains, inconsistencies, cracks in the picture presented by the old order, without declaring definitely for any new form. His forms of thought ran to paradox, therein remaining true to the Janus-headed character of a man who, having been born at the meeting-point of two eras, has to devote half of himself to each. His scepticism is heard as an undertone through all phases of the coming Rococo. The sceptical attitude lacks the spirit of compromise and conciliation. Similarly all the concrete expressions of the Rococo are lacking in symmetry, the reflection in the glass which reconciles opposites; it was essentially asymmetrical. What the philosopher thought out in the brain, the Rococo artist drew in subtle lines—for Rococo art was linear—both expressed only potentialities, not any clear conclusion. The essay became the dominant literary form. Even colour lost the firm clearness of the Baroque. The Rococo was fond of pale tones, gradations without sharp definition. Porcelain, which lends itself to light and delicate gradations of colour, became the typical material of Rococo art.

In this subtlety of feeling lies the secret of the affinity in style of Rococo and ancient Chinese culture. It was not so much the written word which gave the Rococo its conception of China. Sublimated in the delicate tints of fragile porcelain,

25

in the vaporous hues of shimmering Chinese silks, there revealed itself to the minds of that gracious eighteenth-century society in Europe a vision of happy living such as their own optimism had already dreamed of. What could that gracious, charming society find in the severe political morality of the North Chinese Kung? The soft, plastic culture of Southern China, where in the fantastical valley of the Yang-tze the mystical blossom of Laoism flourished, where the tea-like fragrance of Zennism ravished the souls of men, this it was which, lurking in the gleam of the porcelain of Kwang-si and in the soft rustling folds of silks from Fu-kien, aroused all the delight and admiration of that European society which, without being conscious of these inner affinities, was itself the nursery of an intimate culture in fullest bloom. France, the native soil of this Rococo culture, accordingly loved the many-coloured Chinese porcelains, while Holland and England, to whose more frigid temperament this ware did\ not appeal so strongly, gave the preference, in their importations from the East, to the plain blue and white porcelain, which was at the same time less graceful in its forms.*

Le Comte in his work on China, 1699,[1] mentions three kinds of porcelain: the yellow imperial, the grey ' crackly,' which he personally considered the finest, and thirdly the kind which most appealed to the general taste of Europe, the many-coloured porcelain—" white, painted with figures of flowers, trees and birds—of the kind we have in Europe." And the soul of this Jesuit Father was vexed by the undiscriminating eagerness with which the traders of the West bought up the coloured porcelain: " But the European

---

* Up to the fourteenth century only monochrome porcelain in very pale tints had been produced in China. And Chinamen of taste to this day regard the Sung and Yüan dynasties as the best period for porcelain. It was not till the fifteenth century that the Chinese became acquainted with the ' Mohammedan blue,' which was probably brought to them by the Arabs. Porcelain was then painted under the glaze with blue on white. Later on, in the seventeenth century, it was usual to paint in three or five colours over the glaze. It was from the province of Kwang-si, or alternatively from Arita, where the blue porcelain painted under the glaze was mainly produced, that the Europeans, according to their taste, obtained the many-coloured, and the blue and white china respectively. It may be noted here that Imari, where the blue Arita ware was shipped, was after 1641, like all Japanese ports, only open to the Dutch trade.

merchants no longer deal with good artists, and, having no knowledge of these matters, take what the Chinese offer them."

While in the seventeenth century porcelain was still treated as a curiosity only displayed in quantity in a few great palaces (in Madrid or Versailles), at about the turn of the century, whether as a result of the immense supply, or of the demands of individual taste, it became an ordinary household necessity, especially when warm drinks, tea among them, had become the fashion. There was a pressing demand for suitable tea-services, and what could be more natural than to look for models in the land where the tea-cult had its origin ? But as the Chinese and Japanese use only handleless cups, special cups with handles were made for European use. Often, too, white porcelain was ordered for this purpose, to be painted in Europe according to the special tastes of the purchaser.

But, alongside of this practical use of porcelain, the use of it as an ornament still continued. One thinks of the fantastic plans of Augustus the Strong for his ' Indian Pleasure-house,' now Pillnitz, where, according to Wackenbarth, something quite new and strange, such as had never been seen either in Welsh-land (*i.e.*, Italy) or elsewhere, was to be created. " Walls, ceilings, window-recesses, and the like were panelled with porcelain."[2] The pediment group on the ' Japanese-Meissen ' palace, as Wackenbarth called that grace-ful building, made Augustus the recognized patron and protector of porcelain production, native and foreign. The king actually conceived the Bizarre and thoroughly Rococo idea of having tables and chairs made of porcelain.[3] Thus it fell to the lot of Saxony to be the elaborator of this porcelain-Rococo. From 1710, was carried on in Meissen the earliest European manufacture of hard-paste white porcelain. To trace the history of all the changes in style, and all the experiments made in the attempt to imitate Chinese porcelain, would be an attractive task, but would outrun the limits of the present treatise. It is indispensable, however, that we should follow in outline the development which, through the inventive genius of Meissen, bore such rich fruit for the Rococo culture of which we are speaking.

Already about the year 1540, the Venetians had begun to produce majolica decorations with blue arabesques ' *alla* *porzellana.*' In Florence, under Francesco Maria (1574–84), attempts to imitate Chinese hard-paste porcelain had had, for a time, a certain success in the so-called ' Medici porcelain,' a kind of stone-ware with glass frit.   They finally arrived at a sort of faïence which, like the Venetian majolica, was painted in dark blue on a white or bluish (*smaltino*) ground.   Curiously enough, this kind of decoration exactly corresponded to that which was in fashion at the time in China.   From Venice the faïence was transplanted to Dutch soil at Delft.   There, as the secret of the true porcelain was still undiscovered, it was attempted to perfect the native milky-blue clay-ware, which had been manufactured in Holland since 1625, so that it should more and more resemble the Chinese porcelain.   Accordingly it was mainly the Chinese model which stimulated the manufacture of faïence at Delft to its highest efforts; and, again, it was the example of Delft which prompted the development, beginning about the middle of the seventeenth century, of the faïence industry in the rest of Europe.   The colouring generally goes back to Chinese models. (Figure 1.)   " Processions of Chinese with long pigtails and umbrellas, the Mandarins in palanquins."   Sometimes we find set in a charming landscape Buddhist gods of Chinese type, such as the big-bellied Pu-taï; parks with pavilions, fantastic beasts alternating with plants in Chinese style (chrysanthemums and cherry-blossom). In the treatment we find all sorts of misinterpretations of Chinese motives.   For example, the well-known Meissen ' onion-pattern ' is a perversion of an original Chinese pine-apple motive. (Figure 2.)   Or again, Chinese bird's-eye perspective representations of bridges with broken lines produced on the European eye, unused to such bridge-forms, the effect merely of a decorative zigzag line.   On numerous Delft plates of the seventeenth century such zigzag lines are to be seen labelled ' au tonère,' which can only be explained in this way.   The Dutch influence spread first to France (Nevers, Rouen, St Omer) and then to Germany (Nürnberg, Fulda, Bayreuth).   It became of quite special importance when at last, in 1709, Böttger of Meissen succeeded in producing the first genuine European porcelain.*

* According to the latest researches it appears to be questionable whether Böttger was actually the inventor of European porcelain. Along with his name that of the naturalist Ehrenfried von Tschirnau is mentioned as having been the real discoverer. The question has

Böttger, an ' alchemist ' by profession, had come to Dresden
in 1707. Although (or, perhaps, because) he had had to flee
from Berlin, Augustus the Strong took him under his pro-
tection. Böttger promised to produce porcelain, and the
king provided him with a laboratory. He actually succeeded in carrying out his promise. In 1709 the first genuine
hard-paste porcelain came from his furnace. In 1710 the
manufacture was removed to Meissen, and, as early as 1714,
it was able to send porcelain to the Leipzig fair. In 1717
it had its first successes with the blue ware. The faïence-
manufacture had by this time amassed a considerable stock
of Chinese motives which was now further enriched and
enlarged in imitation of Chinese models. Porcelain was
regarded as a gift from the Chinese world, and it was only
natural that the Chinese manner of painting should be taken
as a model. The painter Herold, an exile from Vienna, added
polychromatic decoration to the achievements of the Meissen
industry; and, from the first tentative experiments with
delicate lace-work ornaments, painted red with gold and
purple lustre, there soon developed his gaily coloured Chinese
scenes and his ' Japanese ' sketches of flowers and animals,
with which we are familiar from numerous pieces of that
period. Not only his own paintings, but drawings and
sketches which he prepared for the use of his porcelain-
painters, bear the impress of this curious cross-bred
Chinoiserie, in which European ideas of form were coupled
with Chinese motives.*
The technique of porcelain-painting was soon so widely

---

not yet been settled, and, therefore, the traditional view has been
retained here.   But, even if these fresh researches should prove correct,
it would in no way alter the fact that it was from Böttger's factory
that the first European porcelain of any note was placed *on the market*.
   * In those days people could only think of porcelain in connexion
with China.   In England it was actually called ' china,' and is still
so called.   Indeed, when at a later time a brilliantly white and plastic
kaolin was discovered, it was called ' china-clay.'   The English could
never bring themselves to use the Portuguese word ' Porcelain,'
although it very curiously and strikingly describes the thing.   The
history of the word is as follows.   The Portuguese, the first Europeans
to reach the Far East, found in the East Indies certain mussel-shells
which were used, as they were in China also, as coins.   On account
of their shape and rosy colour, the Portuguese called them *porzella*
or ' little pigs.'   Then they came upon crockery-ware, the material
of which looked so like the shells, that they coined for it the word
' Porcelain.'

known, that the practice arose of taking Chinese porcelain and adding to it special decoration to suit the idiosyncrasies of European taste. We have spoken already of the importation of white porcelain to be painted in Europe. Alongside of this practice, grew up the so-called ' Japan ' technique. According to Savary's great trade *Cyclopœdia*, in the first half of the eighteenth century the Dutch and English were clearly in the habit of importing the cheaper blue-on-white porcelain from China itself, while the dearer polychrome (*Arita*) porcelain was brought from Japan. The latter appealed especially to the taste of Europe in those days, and better prices were to be got for it. The European merchants were no more honest than the Chinese, and were familiar with Eulenspiegel's trick of wrapping a cat in a hare's skin and selling it for a hare. So they simply painted up their cheaper blue-on-white porcelain in the taste of the times with a little red, threw in a few flowers and threads of gold, baked it again, and sold the resulting produce as ' genuine ' *Arita* porcelain.

But there were other and more tasteful ways in which, especially in France, imported Chinese ware was finished in Europe. Bronze mountings were fitted especially to dark-coloured vases, which were used, after the Chinese fashion, for keeping tea in, so that it might not lose its fragrance, or, also after the Chinese manner, as incense-burners—in the French phrase '*Brûle parfums*.' The author himself possesses such an incense-burner with bronze mountings in the style of Caffieri, which in form closely resembles a Chinese incense-burner of proved antiquity to be seen in the Folkwang Museum at the Hague. It appears that in Rococo *salons* they had adopted, among other Chinese customs, that of mingling the scents of incense and of tea.

A little story, for which Savary vouches, throws a curious light on the workings of that spirit of inventiveness, or of rediscovery in the field of minor artistic production which makes Rococo art so interesting. He tells how a certain man succeeded in imitating the painted Chinese mirrors. " The figures and designs are not carvings or paintings laid on to the completed mirror. The technique is so difficult that I doubt whether there are two persons in France who understand it. When I was in Port Louis, in 1745, I saw a Chinese mirror, which had been sent to the Marquis de Roturier, whereon was seen a Chinese lady at her toilet; above her in one corner was a parrot on its perch, and, behind it, a monkey. Overcome by the beauty of the mirror and the skill of the workmanship, I tried eagerly to discover by what means I could imitate it. When, after much careful thought, I believed I had solved the problem, I secured the help of Monsieur Desnoyers, manager of the magazine at the citadel of Port Louis, who was a very skilful painter. Together we worked out my idea and had the happiness to achieve a result which seemed to both of us highly satisfactory. This is what one must do in order to imitate these curious productions of China."[4] Then follows a detailed account of the technique.

However, among all the crafts introduced in those days from China, the treatment of porcelain easily took first place. For Saxony the new industry became within a short period one of the richest sources of income. And when Frederick the Great, in the Seven Years' War, laid his hand on Saxony, he made use of the Meissen porcelain for the payment of his debts. He sent, at that time, to the Countess von Camas a small porcelain snuff-box as a present, and, in the letter which accompanied it, he wrote: " I send you, dear little mother, a trifle to keep you in mind of me—I have been ordering porcelain here for all the world—indeed that brittle material is now my only wealth. I hope that those to whom I send such presents will take it as hard cash, for we are as poor as beggars; nothing is left us but honour, our sword and porcelain."[5] And, at an earlier time, during the second Silesian War, he once wrote to Fredersdorf, his Privy Chamberlain: " I am sending porcelain to the figure of 100,000 Reichsthaler to Berlin. Out of it I intend to pay Koz-kows-ki* and to sell to the value of 50,000 Reichsthaler. Only see that we get rid of it."[6]

It would be impossible to enumerate all the countless collections of porcelain contained in the Chinese cabinets of all the little Rococo palaces. At most, one can mention a few characteristic examples, such as the Chinese apartments in the Ludwigsburg palace in Schönbrunn, the Mirror Cabinet in the old royal palace in Munich (one of the ' rich chambers '

* Stimulated thereto by the successes of Meissen, the king had, in order to improve the financial position of the kingdom, acquired for 225,000 Rthlr. from the merchant Gotzkowski his Berlin porcelain factory (afterwards the Royal Porcelain Manufactory).

destroyed by the fire of 1729), the Mirror Room in the palace
at Ansbach, the ' Porcelain Room for Cavaliers ' in the same
place.   In the case of the palace of Monbijou in Berlin (afterwards the Hohenzollern Museum) an old guide-book is in
existence which gives information about the originally
elaborate decorations ' *à la chinoise*.'   Although several of the
details contained in it should rightly be introduced later, when
we come to treat of Architecture, we give the inventory here
as a good example.   The following Chinese articles are
mentioned: " . . . 6, Concert-room with Chinese hangings
in paper; 10, the Fer-à-cheval Chamber (so-called on account
of its horseshoe shape): the walls are lined with woodwork,
the painting in the Chinese taste divided up into compartments; 12, a gallery: yellow hangings in Chinese taste with a
border carved in wood . . . in the one-storeyed building in
the garden, enlarged and embellished by the now widowed
queen (Friderica), are a number of fine rooms, for the most
part newly and very tastefully decorated and furnished;
4, a room with rose-coloured hangings, on which are landscapes painted in Chinese taste in compartments; 6, a cabinet,
and 9, a chamber with Chinese hangings in paper; 11, a chamber
black-lacquered in Chinese taste; 20, the queen's bedroom with
silken Chinese hangings: the alcove is *boursé* blue and gilt;
23, a cabinet of Chinese hangings; 24, porcelain gallery:
green-lacquered woodwork adorned with gilded carving.
Here is seen a quantity of Chinese porcelain; Japanese and
Berlin porcelain over the window arches; 27, Chinese hangings
framed with mirror glass; 34 and 35, a hall and gallery with
hangings in Chinese taste with fine carvings."   In addition,
those rooms in Monbijou are deemed worthy of special
mention which the great king caused to be furnished with costly
porcelain for his mother, Sophia Dorothea, during her widow-
hood.   How many Chinese rooms have suffered the same
fate as those of Monbijou and have been transformed by the
taste of a later age (Empire, *e.g.*) !   In the furnishing of all
these private apartments Rococo taste gave the first place
to porcelain.

Anton Springer is mistaken when he says[7] that we have to
thank the silversmith for the ' *style rocailleux*.'   Equally
mistaken are the observations appended by Fr. Sarre to
Springer's statements: " This is the metal which corresponds

to the real character of Rococo much rather than porcelain, which is widely regarded as the characteristic vehicle of the style and to which its development has been ascribed. In silver the forms suggesting leaves and mussel-shells can easily be worked up by the craftsman from the curved surface—they fit it as it were; whereas, in porcelain, the material in its unfired state itself forbids too bold a play of forms, so that it requires to be painted and gilded before it can show the proper sharpness of definition." In answer to this it has to be said that a ' bold play of forms ' is precisely what porcelain permits—one has only to think of the magnificent porcelain chandelier in the audience-room of the Ansbach Palace, presented formerly to the Margravine by Frederick the Great; also, that to produce sharply cut lines in porcelain is eminently possible, as can be proved from numerous examples. Silver, on the contrary, lacks many of the qualities which porcelain certainly possesses, and which it most perfectly impressed on the general style of the Rococo *salon*—the delicacy of tone, for instance, and the exotic suggestion which made it so peculiarly *chic* and so desirable to Rococo society.

It was porcelain, the symbol of the brilliancy, the colour, the dainty sentiment, peculiar to the Rococo, which inspired such verses as the following:[8]

> " *Allons à cette porcelaine*
> *Sa beauté m'invite m'entraine.*
> *Elle vient du monde nouveau,*
> *L'on ne peut rien voir de plus beau.*
> *Qu'elle a d'attraits, qu'elle est fine !*
> *Elle est native de la Chine.*"

But the influence of Chinese artistic production on the development of the Rococo was not limited to the discovery of porcelain. The Rococo, with its fresh feeling for artistic things, made fresh demands on the materials of art. How well porcelain met these requirements should be clear from the foregoing pages. In regard to materials, lacquer perhaps comes next after porcelain. It was not by chance that the acquisition of this further craft, the preparation of lacquer, from the—in regard to arts and crafts—far more advanced East was achieved by the Rococo; and, as proof of the relationship between the two materials, we may point to the fact that porcelain ware with a lacquer-like appearance, being painted in black and gold, the typical colours of lacquer-work, was at the time extremely popular. During the seventeenth century complete Chinese lacquer cabinets were already being imported into Europe, especially for the French court, in considerable number.[9] It is not certain whether it was as a matter of fact the Augustine monk Eustachius who first brought the secret of lacquer to Rome. What is certain is that the first results of any value in the imitation of Chinese lacquer were achieved towards the end of the seventeenth century in France.

Lacquer, which in the time of Louis XIV had still been regarded as a special rarity, soon became so common in all possible forms that the excessive use of this fine ware already aroused the economic wrath of the elder Marquis de Mirabeau.[10] The inventories of his time contain numerous remarks on East Asiatic *Importanda*, among which Chinese lacquer, *vernis la Chine*, or, even as early as this, French imitations bearing a Chinese mark, are frequently met with.* In the daybook of the merchant Lazare Duveaux, an invaluable source for such researches as these, ' *curiosités vernies* ' are mentioned on almost every page.[11]

The lacquer industry in France, which in this matter took the lead in Europe, soon came to centre round the work of the Martin family. The most important of the four brothers of this name, who exercised the craft of *vernisseur* with distinguished success, Robert Martin, enjoyed the special favour of La Pompadour. She liked his graceful flower and bird decorations on a dark lacquer ground, which he took from Chinese and Japanese models (Figure 3), and, in 1752, gave him large orders for her palace of Bellevue. We find her name at this period in Duveaux' daybook at the head of long lists of every sort of lacquer-work.

As early as 1730 French lacquer was able to compete with that of Eastern Asia. Its fame soon spread beyond the frontiers of France: Fredrick the Great carried off the son of Robert Martin to his court as *vernisseur*. And Voltaire, the admirer of East Asiatic culture and civilization, gave

* The French vessel *Amphitrite*, whose voyages to China, on the special behalf of the Government, were treated by the Parisians as affairs of national importance, brought back on its second journey (1701–3) a whole cargo of lacquer, so that for some time to come all lacquer went by the name of ' *vernis la Chine Amphitrite*.'

expression in *Les Tu et les Vous* to his delight over this last achievement of French industry in the words:

" *Et les cabinets où Martin*
A surpassé l'art de la Chine."

But the use of lacquer was not limited to house-furniture. It was applied also to palanquins on the Chinese model. Later again these ' sedan-chairs ' were mounted on wheels, and in this way the ' chaise ' originated, whose development out of the palanquin is still traceable both in material and form.

About the beginning of the seventeenth century the closed palanquins of Oriental pattern were introduced into Europe. In 1644, they are mentioned as the ' latest novelty ' by the author of *Les lois de la galanterie*. One is reminded of Molière's reference to them in several of his comedies, especially in certain passages of *Les précieuses ridicules* of 1659. It was during the century in which the spirit of Absolutism, with its sharp sense for distinctions of rank, prevailed in Europe, with the ' *roi soleil* ' for its centre, that this symbol of the strictly hierarchical social order of the Far East reached the height of its popularity. Even the idea of issuing special regulations for sedan-chairs was taken from China. In Vienna, for example, bearers were strictly forbidden to accept as passengers " sick persons, lackeys, and in particular Jews."[12] The Emperor used to be carried in a palanquin of special magnificence. Palanquins varied in form and colour, in order that the rank of the passenger might be recognized.* In old-world Nürnberg, a sedan-chair order was issued by the town authorities as late as 1861. By that time, of course, most of the sedan-chairs had been consigned to the lumber-room, whereas the records from the early years of the eighteenth century speak of the crush of chair-carriers outside churches and theatres. There was a regular rage for sedan-chairs. The Duchess of Namur (†1707), for example, used to have herself conveyed in her chair every year to her country-seat of Neufchâtel; forty French ' coolies ' followed her in carts, ready to take their turn as bearers. In this way she

* Vienna ordinances of the year 1727 distinguish, *e.g.*, " Court and Privy Council *porte-chaises.*" The differentiation by colour was an imitation of the Chinese ordinance which allowed the Emperor alone to use a yellow palanquin, while all others had to be black.

would make the journey of 130 miles in ten or twelve days. The Archbishop of Cologne of the day was also in the habit of going in a chair to visit his diocese; and at the height of the Rococo period in Germany the custom spread to the remotest corners of every petty principality. Pure matter of fashion as it may appear, there was, none the less, an inner significance in these external trifles.

At a time when in Germany and Austria the sedan-chair habit was still on the increase, people were already getting tired of them in France. The chair-regulations did not fall in with the more free and easy manners of the Regency. In 1737 only the 'lesser people' continued to use chairs: the well-to-do rode in chaises.

And the fact that it was at this particular period that the change from 'chair' to 'chaise' took place has a certain interest. A curious historical detail throws some light upon it. In Japan it was customary for chairs to be mounted on wheels and drawn by horses; and the Dutch had long before this attempted unsuccessfully to imitate them.[13] The inference is easily drawn that the French *chaises* were the first successful imitations of the Japanese.

The practice of the many-sided art of lacquering was not confined to France. England, Holland, and Venice were the first to follow her example. It would take us too long to go in detail into the history of lacquer-work in Europe. One episode only shall be related because it lies near home. It would hardly be worth while to touch on the history of the Stobwasser lacquer-manufactory of Brunswick but for certain interesting details which it offers. Young Stobwasser had come, obviously by accident, into possession of French recipes for lacquer. In 1757 he succeeded in producing the first good lacquers. It should be explained that before this he had been helping his father, who carried on in Ansbach a business with Prussia, and that the Stobwassers of Ansbach were in the habit of stocking lacquered canes, which Frederick the Great had introduced into the Prussian army. Now that young Stobwasser was able to produce lacquers for himself he began both to paint and to lacquer his sticks, using Chinese models with landscapes and Chinese figures. He also imitated especially the Japanese gold lacquer.[14] Gradually he deserted the Oriental models. In 1763 he settled

finally in Brunswick and founded there a privileged lacquer-
factory. The Stobwasser lacquered snuff-boxes became
famous all over the world. Soon he went on to making his
things of papier mâché after the Oriental fashion, and in this
way he superseded the technique till then usual in Germany—
practised, *e.g.*, in Augsburg since 1700—of lacquering on
wood. In this way every mature art, even such a minor art
as this, always in the end finds out its true material. Indeed,
the artistic feeling of a period itself determines what materials
shall be employed in its service, selecting those which are most
akin to its own character. We have seen how the arts of
lacquer and of porcelain sprang up out of the Rococo feeling
for style. We shall next discover that it was only in the
Rococo time that the art of handling silk, though it had long
been practised in Europe, first attained its wide extension
and reached a refinement which it had perhaps never attained
previously, and has not since attained.

The growth in the demand for silk at that period will be
best shown by sketching very shortly the history of silk-
importation, and incidentally we shall see how these imports
influenced the European industry. During the whole of the
Middle Ages silk was used only in limited quantities; during
the Renaissance its use was extended even beyond the borders
of Italy. In the seventeenth century an enormous increase
in the importation of silk from the East took place, and, as
the importation lowered prices, a great increase also in the
use of it. The fairs were glutted with silks. The fabulous
prices which could be obtained stimulated the trade in an
ever-increasing degree. The sale-books of the *Compagnie
des Indes Orientales* of May 28, 1691, show that muslins which
had cost in the East 327,000 livres were sold for 1,267,000 livres;
silks bought for 32,000 livres were sold for 97,000 livres.[15]
And at a considerably later date, when competition had
sensibly lowered prices, Savary could still write: " The
province of Che-kiang in China is the greatest producer of
silk in the world. It is believed to produce as much as all
Europe and Asia combined. What is told of the quantities
of silk manufactured there seems scarcely credible. The
profits to the purchaser amount to at least 100 per cent."[16]
Indeed, he says it was possible for Europeans to make 200 per
cent. if they bought direct in Nanking and so eliminated

the Chinese middlemen and the Indian traders. Clever
merchants calculated, he says, that silk which had cost a
hundred dollars in Nanking could be sold even in Canton for
one hundred and fifty and in Siam for almost three hundred
dollars.[17]   To show how much profits stimulated importation
into Europe, we will quote what Raynal says under the year
1772: " Last century, the Europeans brought very little silk
from China (*i.e.*, by comparison with the continually increasing imports of the eighteenth century); our own sufficed
for the black and coloured shawls which were then in use;
the taste of the last forty, and more particularly of the last
twenty-five years, for white and bright-coloured shawls has
caused an ever-increasing demand for the productions of China.
The consumption has recently risen to 80,000 yearly, of which
France alone takes three-quarters.   In 1776 the importation
has increased so greatly that the *Compagnie d'Angleterre* alone
imported 104,000." What is here stated of the consumption
of these articles in France is true of Europe generally.   Paris
was already the centre of European fashion.   From Paris
Austria, Italy, and England in particular, were supplied with
large doll mannikins, dressed in every detail to exhibit the
latest fashions; and we may see how war used to be carried
on in those days from the fact that this trade was never inter-
rupted during the War of the Spanish Succession, so that the
foreign orders—those from Austria, for example—contributed
even during the war to the prosperity of the French
industry.[18]

For the flourishing condition of its silk-industry, both on the
artistic and the technical side at the end of the eighteenth
century, the French were indebted to the impulse given by the
uninterrupted importation of Chinese materials during the
seventeenth century (Figure 4 and Figure 5).   The hand-
painted silks from the East dominated the fashion during the
second half of that century.   In 1669, the first French ship,
the *Saint Jean Baptiste*, had come home from East India
carrying a cargo of Chinese silks; and soon after this, in 1672,
Le Mercure galant introduced the fashion for ' *robes indiennes*.'
" Skirts ' *à la Psyche* ' are always fashionable, as are mantles
of Indian material."[19]   By 1673 the Chinese fashion had been
so far ' democratized ' that, as a substitute for the expensive
hand-painted silks, printed stuffs were already being supplied.

Le Mercure galant writes in reference to this: " Lately, however, they have been printing materials which are almost as beautiful as the painted ones, but the first that were printed were only for the trimming-makers; they made printed taffetas also, in place of which satin is now preferred. This is so fine that it is difficult to tell whether one is looking at printed or painted material."[20] And in July, 1677, the same periodical contains a witty conversation on the fashions, in the course of which Clarissa says to her friend: " What is one to do? One has to paint oneself from head to foot to keep in with the fashion. They will soon, I expect, be copying the Iroquois, who paint their faces all the colours of the rainbow !"

In view of the ever-increasing consumption of such painted or printed silks, the already well-established French industry naturally endeavoured to meet the demand itself. This meant a simultaneous hostility to Chinese importation.

At once a number of silk-factories introduced changes to meet the Oriental tastes of their customers. In France, Holland, and Flanders special factories were set up for the painting or printing of textiles ' *à la mode indienne.*'[21] But it was of little avail that they put this mark or ' *à la Chine* ' on the home-made products. A contemporary observed: " The manufacturers of Paris, Tours, and Lyon, in order to flatter the national taste, undertook to supply a patterned silk or satin material, in imitation of the first Chinese dragon-patterns. . . . Some of the imitations were very fine; but they obtained only a moderate sale, both on account of their prices, which were considerably higher than those of the genuine ' dragons,' and by reason of the prefer-ence for the foreign materials. It hardly looks as if the French could be cured of this."[22]

Accordingly the Regency endeavoured, by limiting or actually prohibiting imports from the East Indies, to come to the support of the French industry. After the death of Colbert (1683), Louvois continued this policy. In 1686 he wrote to the President and Director of the *Compagnie des Indes orientales*, Marquis de Seignelay, that measures must be taken to prevent " the importation of textiles on the large scale hitherto usual. Influence must be brought to bear on the trade so that the return-cargoes shall be made up

partly of silks, and partly of other precious wares." De
Seignelay received at the same time a memorandum from
Lesieur Chauval de Dieppe containing the complaints of the
manufacturers. In 1686 Louvois issued an order prohibiting
all importation whatsoever of painted silks from the East.
In 1691 followed the prohibition of ' *mousselines* ' and ' *toiles
blanches.*'[23]

But these laws do not seem to have been strictly admin-
istered. In 1695, for example, we find the *Compagnie des
Indes Orientales,* which was always the pampered child of
the French government, obtaining authority to import
painted stuffs during the following three years, with the
significant addition: " and longer, if it so please His Majesty;
up to a maximum of 1,500,000 livres in the year, with the
reservation that the Company shall re-export them at its own
expense, and shall not be permitted to sell them to His
Majesty's merchants."[24] That is, the permission was to
apply only to transit-trade. But a strict control of the sales
was obviously impossible.

And in 1792, the Deputies of Lyon, speaking in the name of
Lyon, Tours, Paris, Nîmes, Reims, Amiens, and other cities,
complained of the damage inflicted on them by this East
Indian or Chinese fashion. The artisans of these cities could
get no work and were obliged to go abroad. They petitioned
for a fresh interpretation of the edict of 1664,[25] in the sense
that the *Compagnie des Indes Orientales* should have the sole
right to import East Indian goods, *with the exception of* " *silk
stuffs and painted cloths.*"[26]

How imperfectly these prohibition-orders were carried out
is shown by the fact that, from the year 1700 onwards, the
Compagnie de la Chine was having embroideries and complete
garments made in China on European models, of which the
Amphitrite brought home the first consignment in 1700.[27]

But it was smuggling which more than anything else
deprived the laws of their effect. Importation by way of
England and Holland went on without interruption. Once,
when the French Chamber of Commerce was deliberating as
to how they could regulate the sale of the limited quantities
of material of which the importation was permitted by way
of experiment, they came to the conclusion that they could
rely neither on the *Commis de ferme* nor on the police, since

both were interested in the smuggling trade.[28] Here again
the system of exclusive legislation proved its inadequacy.
The Abbé Raynal severely criticized the ' *politique protection-
niste* ' of the French government: " Everything that came
from India," he wrote, " was continually overloaded with
duties. Six months seldom passed without the appearance
of orders permitting, or prohibiting, the use of these goods;
it was a perpetual see-saw of contradictions in a branch of
the administration demanding well-considered and consistent
principles."[29]

This was quite in accordance with the state of the central
government of France in the eighteenth century, choked as
it was with papers, privileges, and prohibitions, whose contents nobody knew and nobody paid any attention to. Thus
it came about that even in the 1759–1769 edition of the
Dictionnaire Universel under the heading ' *Etat des marchan-
dises étrangères de quelque pays que ce soit, dont l'entrée est
défendue dans toute l'étendue du royaume* ' are included the
painted silks from China—" stuffs or druggets of dyed or
painted material on pain of confiscation and a fine of 3,000
livres, in accordance with the resolution of November 22, 1689.
Stuffs from India, China, or the Levant, painted or dyed
cloths, even muslins and white cottons, except such as are
imported by the *Compagnie des Indes*,[30] on pain of confiscation
and other penalties as determined by the order of August 2,
1729, according to the amount of the offence."[31]

It is in print that contracts, decisions of the courts, Acts
of Parliament, and the like are longest preserved, because
copies are easily multiplied. Long after real life has shaken
off such restrictions, their ghosts continue to haunt the
handbooks. So it was in the case of the importations from
the East. The life of the Regency drove its coach-and-four
through all the prohibitions; and, impossible though it be
to trace all the technical and stylistic influences at work,
certain points can be made out with sufficient clearness.

Weaving, for example, has always occupied a special place
in artistic industry. Textiles have been, from time im-
memorial, a very important article of world-commerce—we
cannot enter here into the reasons of this; and this lively
interchange of products led to a simultaneous interchange
of artistic motives. But, on the other hand, weaving as an

D

industry was preserved from any very capricious changes at least as late as the end of the eighteenth century; so that a certain steadiness in the development of its forms makes possible a broader treatment of the subject. This slowness of movement was due to the fact that it was technically bound to its mechanism. Thus, weaving may be taken as a ' typical ' craft, and as such will reflect, more truly than any other, the style of a period, so far as it was at all able to adapt itself thereto. The degree to which weaving was constrained to work in types is expressed clearly in the lines of its organization as an industry. They reveal a tendency to centralization. The French silk-industry, which was supreme in Europe during the Rococo, had its centre in, and regulated itself on, Lyon. In that city were to be found all the inventive and artistic forces of the industry. Being bound to types, the industry had to rely on the large towns for its customers. The arrangements for selling likewise demanded centralization; for, with the increasing variety in materials produced, the distribution of sales according to districts became a more and more complicated business; and this meant that it could best be directed by one central head. This central position tended, more and more, to be assumed by Lyon; so that, throughout the Rococo, it set the standard even on the artistic side of the industry. In Italy itself, which had borrowed its cultivation of the silkworm from France, and which possessed a successful silk-industry of its own, we have evidence that the fashionable world preferred French silks to the native product. Italians did not consider themselves well-dressed unless they had got their materials from Lyon or Paris. This may be partly due to the fact that their own sense for the decorative had hardly outgrown the Baroque.[32]

The new feeling both for form and for colour, and the corresponding refinement in the technique of weaving, could receive its full development only in the true home of the Rococo, namely, in France. With the change in feeling went a refinement of technique and of textile productions, always under the influence of Chinese models. One is surprised, for instance, by the soft, clinging quality of the French silks of the Rococo in comparison with the Baroque. As the Chinese silks are also distinguished by this quality, we are perhaps justified in assuming that the French borrowed this technical peculiarity along with the Chinese style of ornamentation.[33]

Regarding the influence of Chinese dyeing-technique we have evidence of as early a date as the year 1699.* "The Indians have taught us to produce cotton stuffs, dimity, and muslin, and to print them in fast colours. The dyeing of the Indian cloths has been imitated in Europe, though perhaps not, as regards excellence and strength of colouring, in such perfection as the cloths themselves."[34] The painted satins showed figures of all sorts—men, animals, birds—in imitation of the Chinese. And Savary says: "They tried to imitate the extravagance of the Chinese and Indian patterns, and with success."

In this way, there came to Europe a textile technique by which the colour effects of the silk were notably enriched. They were called simply ' chinas ' after the land of origin. Technically this means that only the threads of the warp are printed with different colours. The result of this process, which Savary calls " one of the most delicate " ever invented, was a blending of the colours, and it was this *nuancé* effect which was felt as so charming.†

In the matter of colours, the Rococo palette was notably enriched by new materials introduced from China. Che-che, the fruit of a leguminous Chinese plant, yielded a peculiarly luminous yellow-gold colour—the colour which figures largely in Rococo decoration. The so-called ' Chinese ' green was obtained from the bark of certain Chinese thorns (*rhamnus*). It has the valuable peculiarity of preserving its beautiful colour even in artificial light. Akin to it was the Lo-Kao, which, nowadays at least, can be produced from European thorns, by the process of Charvin of Lyon.[35]

As a department of the general silk-industry, the embroidering of silk in particular received new directions through Chinese influence. Embroidery-patterns were transformed and multiplied with the help of the Chinese *répertoire* of

* We would point out once more that the term ' Indian ' is not to be taken literally. Dress-materials were often called ' Indian' merely because they had come from China to Europe by way of Indian *dépôts*.

† The Duc de Bourbon had laboratories and workshops erected in the basement of his palace, where, along with lacquer, painted silks on Chinese models were produced, which would bear comparison with the Chinese.

decorative forms (Figure 6). Pillement's flower fantasias would have been unthinkable apart from the Chinese models, and it was Pillement who, through his long residence in that city, obtained such influence on the silk-decoration of Lyon.[36]

Daniel Marot's designs for embroidery, with their bold combination of volutes, lattice-work, and little naturalistic flowers, show such similarity to Chinese motives that influence from that quarter has to be assumed.[37]

Here a parenthesis is necessary in order to prevent misunderstandings. Rococo ornament, of course, grew out of Baroque ornament, and is, in many respects, merely a development of what the Baroque already contained, but it was also led on by Chinese influences—and that is the point which interests us—into lines of its own. Perhaps the right course would be to enquire first how far Chinese motives had already entered into Baroque ornament, but that lies beyond the scope of this work.

With the help of Chinese examples, Rococo embroidery also discovered fresh means of producing those gradations and contrasts of colour which were so much sought after. Gold and silver thread were used chiefly for high lights; to produce the contrasted dull effects, short stitches were employed.[38] To create a brilliant fluidity of surface, low relief with frequent differences in the lie of the thread was resorted to.[39] The fact that, in place of the smooth sewing-silk from Granada till then popular, the embroiderers now more and more preferred the floss silk from Alais, which was so like the Chinese,[40] is, no doubt, another case of Chinese influence. With the new thread they obtained that powdery effect, and that soft, satiny colouring which is seen in perfection in the Rococo pastel-work.

For investigations of this latter kind the inventory of Louis XIV is a rich source. For example, we find mentioned there " Embroideries on blue satin picked out with silver after the manner of porcelain, on a ground of gold material."[41] Obviously this kind of porcelain-like embroidery is to be referred to the model of a certain Oriental material to be found among the imports before mentioned, which had been forbidden by Louis XIV and Louis XV. This was a cotton material with a blue pattern on it, and was for that reason actually called ' pourcelaine.' The colouring was no doubt done by the process which has come into use again with us, the *Batik-Wachsdeck* process, the home of which is the Far East. In the same inventory of Louis XIV, along with actually Chinese embroideries, others in ' *façon de la Chine* ' or ' *à la chinoise* ' are frequently mentioned.[42] Later on special reference is made to stuffs whose flower-decorations are pierced ' *à jour.*' It would seem that this kind of work, which is still produced in China, had been borrowed thence in those days.[43]

From China came too at this time a curious combination of print with embroidery, as well as of painting with embroidery. This latter is actually called ' needle-painting.' It partly took the place of the Gobelin tapestries in the Rococo period. Painters, like François Boucher, provided designs for such embroideries, which often exceeded the Gobelins in size.

The further the Chinese fashion spread, the more pressing became the demand for some material, cheaper than silk, capable of being adapted to this fashion. A Chinese cotton was discovered, printed with brightly coloured flowers, of which the embassy, which Louis XIV sent to Siam, first sent home considerable quantities. This material was imitated without delay and was soon widely used; it was called ' *in- dienne.*' Its production naturally remained mainly a privilege of the English, to whom, by the nature of things, the wool and cotton industries belonged, while the weaving of silk was mostly carried on by the French.

As we have spoken of Gobelins and of Needle-Paintings, and as we are treating of things designed to lend charm to the immediate surroundings of man, this is perhaps the place to say a word about a material which, though it is now completely naturalized among us, was in those days a newcomer, welcomed by the simple citizen as a substitute for the wall-hangings of the well-to-do—namely, wall-paper. In the days of the Rococo, with its fondness for the *intime*, even the ' small people,' as they were called, came to value pleasant interiors. The Chinese wall-papers fell in with the taste of the times, satisfied the demand, and so came to be more and more widely used. In China they had been employed for ages for covering walls and screens. It was the custom there either to paint them or to print them with wood-blocks.

In painting them, water-colours were used. Coloured papers of this kind were imported into Europe from the East in large quantities as early as the seventeenth century. Probably it was the sea-captains who first took a liking to the cheap, gaily coloured stuff and took to pasting it on to the walls of their offices. Soon a wider demand arose, and the first imitations were made with the help of stencils or wood-blocks.

According to unsupported statements, an attempt was made in Rouen as early as 1610 to produce wall-papers with some patterns brought over by missionaries. The first successes really vouched for were obtained by Jean Papillon in 1688. It is possible that he was stimulated to make the attempt by an earlier German example (which, like the French experiments of 1610, went back to Chinese models); for he himself tells of a process, which, he says, was in use in 1638, chiefly in Worms and Frankfurt a. M., where they had manufactured, as a substitute for the costly leather hangings,[44] a gold and silver paper ornamented with conventional flowers.[45]

According to Papillon, Jacques Chauveau and Jean Gabriel Hugian in France attempted to make an improved article. But it was reserved to the English to reproduce a really serviceable wall-paper. In 1746, they succeeded in making primitive blocks 2 metres in length. In 1754, the factory founded by Jackson in Battersea succeeded in making great improvements in the printing. It was there that the first papers with conventional patterns were produced on an industrial scale. They were decorated with landscapes in *clair obscur*, and in the old Chinese manner. In spite of the heavy duties (on every roll of twenty-four sheets), these papers soon had a wide sale in England, and one may find them to this day in old German houses.

In 1786, G. and F. Erhardt founded a factory in Chelsea where wall-papers, silks and linens were printed from the same blocks.[46] The contemporary factory at Sherringham had already sufficient means to attract famous artists of the day such as Brière, Rosetti, Boileau.

In France, as their own papers were not satisfactory,[47] papers on the English model were soon produced. In 1669 the Englishman, Lancoke, obtained permission to erect works in Paris, in which he manufactured, not only papers, but also printed stuffs. After that, it became the practice in France to carry on the two allied industries together.

However, it was not till the French Revolution that all prejudices were removed and that wall-papers were able to attain their present universality.

The delicate tones of porcelain, the vaporous colours of silk, all the things that gave to the Rococo world its charm and grace, are, as it were, enshrined in the paintings of Watteau.

There is nothing to support the idea that Watteau, as a painter, really received any inspiration from Chinese land-scape-painting; but, at the same time, it is difficult not to believe that something of his technique was borrowed from China. This would not be at all surprising in view of the affinity of feeling; and the superabundance of Oriental models would have provided plenty of opportunity. Certain points of connexion may be indicated with caution. Watteau it was who freed French painting from Baroque feeling. He gave it the picturesque as an absolute value, having, inde-pendently of the object, its self-sufficient existence in the beauty of the painting. Poussin and the Louis XIV painters generally had not reached this point. It is the subtle difference which places such a wide gulf between a picture of Watteau's, and the work of the generation which preceded him. Once we forget the content, the figures represented in the pictures, and look only at the colour and form of expression, the secret is revealed: Watteau breathed an in-dependent life into the landscape. We do not find him painting landscapes of the late medieval type, with the canvas divided up by architectural schemes, nor of the sixteenth and seventeenth century Dutch type, with its vivid realism and bright colour. What we find in him is landscape treated as a detached *scena*. As in the Gobelin tapestries the gay doings of a festal world stand out against a broadly-worked landscape-background, so Watteau groups his figures in a landscape which he treats as a back-scene or wall-painting.* To this new valuation of the landscape, the treatment in form and colour corresponds. It is removed to a distance, the forms are nebulous and melt into one an-other, the tone is vaporous and almost monochromatic.

* Richard Hamann somewhere calls this " Nature as tapestry."

Contrasted mountain-forms are painted in subdued colour against a pale blue sky, are partly veiled in clouds—a fairy-story landscape conjured up, one knows not quite how. It had hardly any connexion with the landscape-painting of the past, which used strong colours and made the landscape itself the centre of the picture's life. Not from the Flemings of the sixteenth and seventeenth centuries can Watteau have learnt this.

What we have spoken of above is most strikingly illustrated in Watteau's 'Embarkation for the island of Cythera' (Louvre, Paris). Anyone who has studied closely Chinese landscapes of the Sung period is immediately struck by their affinity with the landscape-background which Watteau has painted here. He was unable to make it unite with the human actors in the scene. His blue distant landscape maintains a separate life of its own. The fantastic forms of his mountains he had never seen with his own eyes: the Flemings had not shown them to him; but they closely resemble the Chinese forms. The darker tone of the contours is Chinese, and so is the curious manner of indicating clouds. The use of monochrome colouring for background landscape, such as Watteau loves, is one of the most prominent characteristics of Chinese landscape-painting. This sentimental treatment of landscape by Watteau already points forward to the pastoral idylls of Boucher and the Nature-worship of his generation; and it is remarkable in this connexion that Chinese landscape-painting likewise had its roots in Nature-worship of a similar kind. Not that this inner affinity was consciously felt by these men of the eighteenth century; such echoes are, as a rule, only perceptible to men of a later generation, who stand further off. What we know is that the men of that age were enraptured by the atmosphere, and by the unusual, somewhat bizarre forms of the Chinese paintings.* They found again in them the delicate tones which they had first met and loved in the porcelain, the brilliance which had charmed them in the silks of China.

But it is not so much the ' great art,' as the numberless prints and drawings of the time of Watteau which illustrate

* Grimm wrote: " Ils (i.e., the Chinese) se piquent dans leurs usages, dans leurs productions, dans leurs actes et dans leurs ouvrages, d'une certaine originalité bizarre, qui non seulement les empêche de copier aucun autre peuple, mais leur défend d'imiter la nature."[43]

our point—the charm which China had for that age. We possess countless works of this kind by Watteau and many others which show actual Chinese motives (Figure 7).

In regard to this it must first be observed that the attitude of these artists towards Chinese painting and drawing was of a peculiarly divided character. The representation of birds and flowers was always admired: " They are very successful with birds and flowers, which they picture with the needle, or on silk hangings so simply that it would be impossible to draw them better from nature."[49] They thoroughly understand all the little and curious details: " They have more sense for the unusual than for real effectiveness in painting."[50] Rococo taste seized upon that which appealed to its own sense of the decorative (*décor*). But of the Chinese drawing of the human form they could make nothing. Eyes trained in the classical (*i.e.*, in the Greek) school could not tolerate what they regarded as a distorted representation of the human figure, such as the Chinese practised. Le Comte pronounces: " It is to be wished that the work which the Chinese apply to the painting of porcelain were more beautiful. . . . The pictures of human beings are all mutilated. They make themselves contemptible thereby in the minds of foreigners; who only know them through this medium, and fancy that they must be as ridiculous and fantastic in real life as they appear in their paintings."[51] But there was great demand for pictures of Chinamen; people wanted to know what they looked like; and so the French artists, and after them the German, made them in their own image. Watteau's Chinese prints are well known.[52] They show us a fantastic world which has little in common with the real China. Watteau's Chinese are really only Europeans in disguise. Take, for example, the one entitled *L'empereur chinois*. It strikes us as a fantastic composition. The emperor with his flower-sceptre—China was looked upon as the flowery land of legend—is seated on a raised structure, under a palm as umbrella, surrounded by a circle of flowery sprays. On one side a Chinese servant is in waiting; on the right two European figures are seen coming to do homage to the emperor.

And this was the character of all Watteau's Chinese engravings: he amuses himself in a charming way with pictures of an imaginary Chinese world, which, if they reveal the idyllic way in which the artist thought of the East, hardly represent what China is or was. And with this dream-world the style of the drawing is in complete correspondence—all delicate airy lines, suggesting rather than delineating. Two panels from what used to be the Hôtel Poulgry in Paris, which are ascribed to Watteau, are described as follows: " Decorative objects scattered over a soft-toned white ground; the colour without being exactly faint, managed with regard to the harmony of the whole, which in accordance with the established convention was of brilliant effect.* The brush-work was light and gay; the brush has flown lightly from point to point like the wings of a bird over flowers." It was no accident that this kind of light and delicate brush-work came to be particularly popular with the ladies of the time, who took up painting in the Chinese manner as a modish form of dilettantism or drew designs after the Chinese on panels and screens.[†53]

Watteau had the good fortune to be enabled to use all his Chinese studies and fantasies on a large scale in the decoration of a cabinet in the palace of La Muette in Paris. He painted all the panelling of this room with *chinoiseries*. But this, the most famous decorative work of the master, which was executed not much later than 1716, had only a brief existence. When d'Argenville visited the palace in 1754, the wall-paintings were no longer there.[55] We now know them only from thirty prints made by Boucher, Jeaurat, and Aubert in 1731 from the originals, immediately after the master's death, and now in the Julienne collection. On the subject of these La Muette paintings, because they are no longer in existence, opinions differ considerably. P. Mainz says: " It needs no saying that these Chinese and Tartars of Watteau's (among them there is actually a woman from Laos) are very much open to criticism on the ethnological side, since Watteau can have had little knowledge of China

---

* This is completely true of Chinese painting also.

† And, again, the painters used to decorate the silk fans of the ladies with all manner of *chinoiseries ;* but of these only a few examples survive. Watteau, for example, painted fans and screens for his lady friends, which have all disappeared.[54] In the Rococo the folding fan, which had been brought to Europe at the beginning of the sixteenth century by a Portuguese brigantine, first became naturalized. In Paris and London Fan-academies, which taught the A B C of fan-language, were numerously attended.

and the neighbouring regions.   Obviously imagination played
a large part in the paintings of La Muette."[56]   On the other
hand, E. de Goncourt is emphatically of the opposite opinion:
" It must not be supposed," he says, " that the *chinoiseries*
of La Muette are merely fanciful.   If Watteau put into these
decorations, as he did into everything he produced, a personal
note, his own artistic conception, the master none the less
prepared himself for his representations of the exotic by
serious study of Chinese things and men."*   Perhaps the
truth lies midway.   We have only one plate of Watteau's
in which a Chinese is drawn from the life.   This study is in
the Albertina Museum in Vienna and bears the name of the
person represented—Tsao; but it may fairly be assumed that
Watteau took advantage of the presence of Chinese in Paris
to get some of them to sit to him for these studies.   On the
other hand, Goncourt overrates their value.

We shall have more to say about Watteau in the sequel
à propos of the *chinoiseries* of some of his contemporaries.
But first a few historical remarks are necessary.

Jules Bérain was still half a prisoner to the stiff convention
of Louis XIV.   But with half his heart he was already at
the head of those whose ebullient fancy had wearied of the
regulation art of the great monarch and who were more and
more breaking away from order, law and symmetry.   Bérain's
freedom of line was the first attempt of decorative art to escape
from the prescribed measure, and to pass from the rather
heavy, pompous style of Louis XIV to the lighter and more
graceful forms of the Rococo.   But what bound Bérain to
the old was the geometrical character of the lines of his back-
grounds.   Herein appear two qualities very characteristic
of the French genius—the sense for the clear and cool, for
law and order (seventeenth century), and the love of the graceful and the incalculable (Rococo).   That, in the Rococo, law
was almost displaced by fantasy, that a stiff profusion was

---

* That, in spite of this, his figures are so comically Europeanized
is a result mainly of the European training of the eye.   For the Chinese
and Japanese are in the same case.   In the Schwerin Museum are
numbers of Japanese paintings on porcelain of the eighteenth century
made after European prints.   They have all taken on involuntarily a
Japanese note.   A representation of Frederick the Great, for instance,
has decidedly Japanese traits about it; in particular, the Mongolian slit
eyes.   On this point the excellent catalogue of this department by
Schlier should be consulted, which can be had on loan at the Museum.

succeeded by a graceful and lively refinement, is explained by the fact that the death of Louis XIV brought with it a relaxation of tension; that, in art, as in all departments of life, etiquette was dethroned. An awakened feeling for nature saw everywhere new things; men dreaded repetition. And symmetry is repetition reduced to the simplest law; it was, therefore, prescribed. Not all at once, but every year more decisively, until Meissonnier broke through the last restraints. And this liberation of decorative art was assisted by the Chinese motives which came to France in all possible forms. China had arrived at its asymmetrical art in much the same way as the Rococo; symmetry was avoided because it involves not only completeness, but repetition. Uniformities in design were regarded as fatal to freshness of fancy.[57] " He makes no order and yet there is no confusion;" this, that is said of Lao Tzŭ by Kung, is true of the spirit of great Chinese art and also of that of the Rococo, to which China stood godmother; " there were decorative objects scattered over a soft-toned white ground."

Gillot (1673–1722) was the first to introduce naturalistic plants and flowers among Bérain's geometric line-work. But with him, as with Bérain, the Chinese figures are foreign elements in the composition. It was Watteau who first made an honest endeavour to place them in a world in which they could feel at home. And in this Watteau's example was followed by others. Christophe Hult painted the famous *chinoiseries* of Chantilly, which were for such a long time wrongly ascribed to Watteau himself. J. Pillement published at Lyon, in 1770, a series of engravings called ' Chinese huts,'[58] which are quite in the style of Watteau (Figure 8), Chinese figures under tiny open shelters, with fantastical palm-trees, airy creepers, one or two arched forms such as people were familiar with in the Chinese bridges, here and there a flower growing—something like what Goethe was thinking of, when in the spring of the following year he wrote:

> " *Kleine Blumen, kleine Blätter*
> *Streuen wir mit leichter Hand,*
> *Gute, junge Frühlingsgötter,*
> *Tändelnd auf ein buntes Band.*"*

---

* Little flowers, little leaves, kind, young Spring-gods, playfully on a coloured ribbon we scatter with light hand.

Of the Rococo artists Boucher is the most successful in producing perfect *chinoiseries* of this kind. From his hand we have, for example, a landscape in dreamy blue, in which are one or two Chinese buildings, in front of them an old man fishing, at his side a Chinese woman gazing pensively into the water, and a small Chinese boy, who holds an umbrella over the old man. Köchlin justly says of it: " All this is excellent, and one can easily understand how it delighted the eyes of those for whom it was intended."[59] Boucher's work was not without its influence on the especial lovers of *chinoiserie*, Pillement and Peyrotte.

And all the painters were imitated in inlay-work, silk-patterns (Lyon), hand-painted and printed stuffs, porcelain and faïence, and on the ' *panneaux décoratifs* ' which were then popular—so that Chinese motives were always meeting the eye.[60] Bérain had already furnished models with Chinese figures for tapestry-borders,[61] Boucher had drawn designs for Chinese hangings for the factory at Beauvais. For the spread of artistic feeling at the period it is a significant fact that such eminent artists were thus able to exercise a decisive influence on all the industries ministering to luxury and ornament, and indeed on the externals of life generally. Printed collections of Chinese ornament, which had a wide circulation, influenced the provincial art-schools of France, which arose out of the *Manufacture Royal des meubles de la Couronne*, and which were particularly flourishing towards the middle of the eighteenth century at the height of the Rococo period.[62] Some of the most widely used of these books of prints may at least be mentioned, in order to give an idea of their contents. Jacques Gabriel Huquier (1695–1772) published a *Collection of more than 600 vases, newly brought together—Books on the various species of birds, plants and flowers of China—Collection of a number of Chinese vases, flowers and symbols of victory—ABC book for those who would learn to draw Chinese ornaments, and other things such as screens, wall-hangings, etc.—Book of stitches for lamp-shades ' à la chinoise.'* In 1735, Fraise brought out a *Collection of Chinese drawings after the originals from Persia, India, China and Japan.* Boucher (1703–1776) published in a collection *Chinese figures drawn by Huquier; other Chinese figures drawn by Ingram; the four elements, Chinese figures*

drawn by Aveline; Chinese tapestries designed by Huquier.
Bellay, about the middle of the century, got Huquier to
make a series of prints, *First collection of designs for wall-
hangings and of fancy drawings for persons interested in
ornament;* similarly Peyrotte, at about the same time, produced a *Collection of Chinese fancy flowers, drawn by Pariset—
Collection of Chinese symbols of victory, drawn by Huquier.*
And Pillement in 1755 brought out in London *A new book
on Chinese ornament.* In Germany one of the best-known
engravers of ornament, P. Decker, published a *Grotesque
Work* of which the designs for lacquer (fire-places, snuff-
boxes, trays) are all *chinoiseries.* Herold, the well-known
porcelain-painter, published plates with Chinese figures; and
Engelbrecht engraved Chinese scenes framed in grotesque
borders, from designs by G. Rogg. The list might be
lengthened indefinitely.[63] But we will end here with a little
anecdote. The Chinese emperor Chien-lung, wishing to
record a successful campaign against the Eleuths in 1759,
caused sixteen sketches to be prepared by his Jesuit painters
in Peking, illustrating the principal scenes of this campaign.
It was his intention to have these sketches engraved in Europe.
—for this art was unknown but much admired in China;
he, therefore, commissioned the Viceroy of Canton to apply
to the English. But, according to a contemporary account,
"Père Le Febvre, who was at the head of the Canton missions,
caused it to be represented to the Viceroy by a mandarin
friend of his, who was a patron of the French, that the arts
were more highly developed in France than in any other
European country, and that engraving in particular had there
reached special perfection. When this was reported to the
emperor, he ordered the sketches to be sent to France "*
(Figure 9 and Figure 10). This was written by the Minister
of State, Bertin, who kept up a lively correspondence with
the Peking missionaries,[64] and what he says of the superiority
of French art in his day is quite true, and may explain why
in these pages we have had more to say of it than even of
our own.

In architecture the development was rather different.

---

* But mention should here be made of the copy made by English
artists of a famous piece of Chinese sculpture. Even in such imitations
the Europeanizing of the forms is clearly to be recognized.

While French architecture preserved, even through the effervescence of the Rococo, the regular dignity and severity of its architectural forms, the lines of which could not be obliterated by any wealth of decoration, it was in Germany that the ' French Grotesque,' as the Rococo was still styled, enjoyed its earliest triumphs.

Here also we have to distinguish between the borrowing of certain organic features of style and playful *chinoiseries*, which, remaining more or less true to style, sometimes even travestying it, were supposed to give a complete presentment of Oriental architecture. In what we have to say we shall endeavour to keep these two things apart.

In France the conflict between the Baroque and the Rococo styles was reflected more strikingly in literature than elsewhere. Obviously this literary feud plays an essential part in the practical composition of differences, which allowed to the decorative element a subordinate life of its own alongside of the architectural scheme, which remained classical. This *via media* was taken by Briseux in particular, who would preserve the old architectural proportions but who, at the same time, claims variety for the decoration.[65] In the art of interior decoration he thinks the greatest effects are produced by a sharp and direct opposition of ' simple ' and ' rich.' In the decorative additions which give character to a room, he thinks a pleasing variety should prevail, such as may be produced without confusion by a happy genius. (" He makes no order, yet is there no confusion.") Brush and chisel in the service of architecture may, he thinks, best seek their models in Nature, which is ever creating new forms without limit. Similarly Cordemoy wished to restore the acanthus in place of the severe and restrained laurel and olive motives, because—and his reason is to be noted—the acanthus in nature forms sweeping and elastic convolutions.[66] These new views, moderate as they are, encountered opposition from the classical tradition. The opposition always centred in the Academy of Paris. The elderly Blondel upheld this point of view without any reservation. He was convinced that architecture was going to the dogs because the younger architects were leaving out of sight the fundamental principles of the art. Blondel and Boffrand also maintained against Briseux the opinion that it was quiet, easy transitions which were to be aimed at in decoration, and not violent contrasts.

But, in opposition to these conservatives, there soon grew up a school, under the leadership of Meissonnier, which went far beyond Briseux. And it is significant, as supporting what was said above of the development of German and French architecture, that his ideas had practical results only in Germany. Generally speaking his demand for an unreposeful breaking up of all symmetry in all departments of architectural activity was rejected in professional circles.

One is tempted to see a connexion between this opposition of two generations of architects and the view of Chinese architecture taken by Europeans, which must surely, one supposes, have played some part in the conflict of styles. Here we are surprised by a curious analogy. While the last generation of the seventeenth century had hardly developed any understanding for Chinese architecture, founded, as it is, throughout on the asymmetrical principle preached by Briseux, in the following generation, taste swung in the opposite direction, and grew into unlimited admiration. This may be illustrated by two typical pieces of evidence. In the book to which we have already referred, Le Comte, who was still firmly rooted in the old French tradition, and who had left France when the Louis XIV style was at its zenith, alludes in the following terms to the Emperor's palace in China: " The whole thing has a sort of magnificence, and strikes one as being the palace of a great prince. But the imperfect idea which the Chinese people has always had of art in general is responsible for certain grave defects even in this work. The apartments are not symmetrically disposed one behind another; in the decorations there is little regularity; one sees nothing of the harmonious arrangement which gives to our own palaces their pleasing and commodious character. Moreover, there is everywhere evidently—what shall I say ?—something unshape (if I may use the expression), which is displeasing to Europeans, and which must be distressing to all who have a feeling for good architecture."[67]

On the other hand, Père Attiret fifty years later, in a letter which had an unusually wide circulation in Europe, expresses a directly opposite judgment on the same Summer

Palace in Peking. "Everything," he says, "in the place is great and truly beautiful, as regards both the design and the execution. And I am the more surprised thereby, since my eyes never yet beheld anything similar to it. . . . In the great variety and multiplicity, which the Chinese give to their buildings, I admire the fertility of their genius. Indeed, I am tempted to believe that, in comparison with them, we are poor and sterile."[68] And in the following passage he defines his impression even more clearly: "With us, uniformity and symmetry are everywhere demanded. Nothing must stand by itself; nothing is tolerated which is the least bit out of its place; one part must be balanced by a corresponding feature on the other side."[69] Clearly Attiret is in the grip of a quite new feeling for style, a feeling which has nothing personal about it, but belongs to his generation. And his generation, apart from the conservatives, judged all art, architecture included, not according to established canons, but solely by the standard of the picturesque (Figure 11). And Chinese architecture was felt as the type of the picturesque. The architectural creations of the Chinese were conceived as part of the landscape, as complementary to the picturesqueness of Chinese Nature, which Père Attiret despairs of describing, saying: "Only the eye can grasp its true content."[70] As a remarkable parallel to this, we will add here the judgment of a modern on the art of the Rococo: "The compositions of Juste-Aurèle Meissonnier and his contemporaries can hardly be described; they must be seen."[71] To what extent this picturesque architecture of the Chinese modified the cognate art of the Rococo can hardly be stated with exactness.*

In the first place, to begin with what is most important, it is not possible to do more than conjecture that the peculiarly pavilion-like ground-plan of Rococo buildings is borrowed from Chinese models, of which this peculiarity is specially characteristic. Of course, in the absence of

* As a curious example of the way in which the Rococo tried to focus all arts under the one view-point of the picturesque, we may quote the phrase of Servandoni, that typical example of Rococo versatility, a rolling-stone who, as architect, painter, organizer, of pageants in Paris, Dresden, Vienna, achieved his last and, as he thought, highest distinction in revolutionizing the opera—" to discover a poetry which shall speak to the eye."[72]

E

concrete proofs, it may always be answered that this peculiar analogy of construction is to be explained by an affinity existing between the architectural feeling of the Rococo and that of the Chinese. Controversy on the subject is useless so long as no clear proof can be adduced. We therefore limit ourselves to cases in which borrowing can be assumed with some certainty. Such influences are most easily established in regard to single architectural features. We will consider first the naturalization of the Chinese roof as a recurrent feature in Rococo architecture.

It is usual to explain the origin of the Western European and the Eastern Asiatic house respectively in the following way: The Asiatic roof was modelled on the tent of the ancient Mongolian-Chinese encampment with its drooping concave surfaces. The form of the tent, made of cloth stretched on poles, can still be recognized even through the modern building material. The Indo-Germanic house, on the contrary, was derived from the ox-waggon; it was this which served as the archetype of the house of Western Asia and Europe. Now the temporary adoption by Rococo architecture of the concave roof-form of the Far East certainly signified an important architectural innovation.*

The reports of the Jesuits had clearly made people believe that the Chinese employed their free asymmetrical style of architecture only for pleasure-houses planted in the midst of gardens, and not for buildings of an official, or representative, character.[73] Accordingly, along with the garden-house, this and various other features of Chinese architecture became naturalized in Europe. We still possess numerous examples of this European-Chinese roofing; but a few German examples may suffice us; many have naturally been removed by a later taste.

One of the most charming specimens of this German Rococo, the palace of Pillnitz on the Elbe, is strikingly

---

* This was the first case in which Western construction underwent considerable influence from the Far East. At an earlier date, in the Gothic, for instance, particular Chinese motives, transmitted partly by way of India, had borne fruit in the West. Among these we may mention in particular the fish-bladder ornament, which had so rich a development in the West, and the origin of which, whether as a form or as a symbol, goes back to the primeval Chinese symbolic figure of the *Tai Yi* (the beginning of all things), which is supposed to signify the mystic unity of Being and Not-Being.

reminiscent of Chinese models. The peculiar construction
of the roof, the lateral pavilions, the flat, elongated, narrow
character of the building are all equally characteristic of
the Chinese pleasure-house. In so accentuated a form these
features were unknown in Europe before that time; and it
is natural to assume that they were in this case borrowed
directly from China.

This view becomes specially convincing when this hybrid
European-Chinese style is compared with the building which,
towards the middle of the century, the Jesuit missionaries
were commissioned to erect in the Imperial gardens at Peking,
the celebrated Summer Palace of Yüan-ming-yüan. The
Jesuits, as European master-builders with European notions
of proportion, were placed in a position similar to that of the
builders of Pillnitz, and the mixture of styles in this Imperial
Palace in Peking is quite comparable with that of Pillnitz.
This precious example of Chinese-European art is unfortunately no longer in existence. When on the occasion of the
Taiping rebellion, which violently opened for Europe access
to the treasures of China, a French expeditionary corps
marched up the Peiho to Peking, the whole structure was,
in October, 1860, utterly destroyed; in reprisal for the
brutal treatment of some European sailors, who had fallen
into the hands of the Chinese, the palace with all its
riches was set on fire. The French commander, Cousin de
Montauban, who sent to Paris the precious things which he
had caused to be snatched from the burning palace, was
decorated by Louis Napoléon with the title of Comte de
Policar, in remembrance of the spot on which he, the country-
man of those Jesuits who a hundred years earlier had
erected that very palace as a token of friendship, had de-
feated the miserably armed Chinese. The appearance of the
building thus destroyed is preserved in numbers of Jesuit
prints. It may be mentioned as a curious fact that Louis II
of Bavaria contemplated a reproduction of the Summer
Palace. In the Cabinet des Estampes in Paris are still to
be seen forty representations of the palace on taffeta, which
the king caused to be made for him. But his plan never
got further than this.[74]

But one of his ancestors, Max Emanuel, had, in his character of genuine Rococo prince, built the ' Pagoda Tower '

in the park of *Nymphenburg*. From France, where he had
lived in exile, he brought back to Munich a taste for the
Chinese. During his residence in Marly and Versailles
there had been much talk of that miniature marvel, the
Trianon de porcelaine, though this had, of course, been
demolished long before by order of Louis XIV.* But Max
Emanuel thought he had a good enough idea of this little
chinoiserie, and it was from this idea that his own design
for the Pagoda Tower was made. It retained, indeed, very
few Chinese features. The blue and white decoration
alone is reminiscent of the *Trianon*, its model. The pavilion
was opened in 1719; and a traveller, who visited the
Nymphenburg in 1781, could still report: "Then on right
and left one sees dragon-fountains with numbers of dragons
and serpents separately represented on rock-work."[76]

With the Pillnitz building, already mentioned, may
perhaps best be coupled the 'Japanese Palace' in Dresden.
Its original name of 'Dutch Palace' indicates that it had
its origin in Dutch architectural ideas. At any rate, there
were multitudes of Dutch workmen employed in the German
building-trade, and it is very possible that some features
of Chinese building reached Germany by way of Holland,
which was, of course, in close touch with the East.† The
palace was built at a rather earlier date than Pillnitz, 1715–
1717, but very soon, 1723–1730, underwent alterations at
the hands of Poppelmann and Jean de Bodt.

The concave Chinese form of roof in Europe, of which
we have only given Pillnitz and the Japanese Palace as
examples, was common in the Rococo, and has in many

---

* *Trianon de porcelaine* was perhaps an imitation of the porcelain
tower of Nanking, which the engravings of Jollien had made famous
as an eighth 'Wonder of the World.' The imitation was naturally
weak, because at the time the engravings were made, about the middle
of the seventeenth century, little was known of Chinese architecture. The façade of the *Trianon*, which was of course a one-storeyed
building, was, for lack of porcelain, covered with faïence. The main
building was surrounded by four pavilions decorated in the same
way. Blue and white were the prevailing colours. This manner of
covering a façade was afterwards known as the '*Façon de pourcelaine*.'
The whole of the interior decoration was also in Chinese taste.
However, as early as 1687, Louis XIV had his own *chinoiserie*
demolished.[75]

† In Holland itself the little palace of Driemond may be mentioned
as an example of such *chinoiseries*.[77]

varieties been recopied from the Rococo in later times even
to the present day.

In and around Potsdam a number of small buildings—
ornamental *chinoiseries* of those days—are still preserved.
In the 'New Garden' is the *Schindelhaus*;[78] at the entrance
to the Avenue, the guard-house and porter's lodge crowned
with a baldaquin; and not far off is the garden-seat roofed
by a Chinese umbrella in lead, with the chains and hanging
ornaments of a pagoda; the point of the roof even has
the nine rings characteristic of pagodas.   The *Tabakscol-
legium* in the Lessing-platz may also be mentioned, erected
by Frederick William I, after the model of a Dutch summer-
house.   It was in Holland that these summer-houses had
first become fashionable; they began there as modest *Koepels*
in the tea-gardens (*thee-tuinen*);[79] The 'Dragon Cottage'
near Potsdam must not be forgotten, built by Frederick
the Great in 1773, near Belvedere, as an experiment for a
pagoda.

In the hunting-box of Stern, in the neighbourhood of
Potsdam, built in 1714, the imitation of another Chinese
motive may be observed in the wide projection of the eaves.
This sprang naturally from the Chinese use of wood as
building material, but was applied in Europe to building in
stone.*   The projecting eaves were lined with wood on the
under side.   In the architecture of the Far East this kind
of building was known as the *Iremoya* roof.   In the hunting-
box at Stern the roof projects a whole metre.   Similar
proportions are seen in the old fortress at Pillau.

Laske, who has made preparatory studies for an enquiry
into the relations of European architecture to that of Eastern
Asia, refers to a number of buildings in Switzerland, which
also display this roof-formation.   They are mostly of the
Baroque and Rococo periods; they stand detached in their
own gardens, having been built as residences by old-estab-
lished families who, in their building, followed the fashion
of the times.   (The examples here referred to must not be
confused with the familiar 'Swiss Cottages,' whose flat
shingle roofs project on quite other principles.)

The sort of way in which the Chinese roof was played

* Very much as in ancient Greece forms, which had their origin in
construction with wood, were transferred to the later stone-architecture.

with as a decorative feature is shown by an existing design from the year 1758 for a water-tower. The turrets of the balustrade are crowned with Chinese umbrella-roofs, supported by wires concealed in scrolls of metal foliage.[80]

This playful adoption of Chinese architectural motives was widespread. With it first begins what we call *chinoiserie*, a term which is always connected with pretty little ornamental work. The quiet naturalization of foreign stylistic elements has nothing to do with fashion, as *chinoiserie* has, is indeed devoid of any truly exotic character, while in the *chinoiseries* it is the exotic which is accentuated. It is worth while to keep the two things distinct. In architecture *chinoiseries* were from the first not generally used but reserved for special purposes, where gaiety of appearance was the first object. The Sinologist, Henri Cordier, who has collected in France rich materials for the study of our subject, found numerous examples, which illustrate this last point. No pleasure-garden with any pretensions to modernity was without its ' Chinese pavilions ' and ' Kiosques.' On the roof of one Parisian hotel there was even a small Chinese garden with two Chinese bridges spanning a small artificial stream.[81]

In Germany, the most successful example of a Chinese pavilion is no doubt the so-called ' Japanese Pavilion ' in the garden of Sans-Souci near Potsdam, belonging to the year 1754. It has not, indeed, completely preserved its original form, in regard to which a contemporary humorously remarks: "We know, at any rate, that the Chinese, though they put pagodas and images of their gods inside their temples, did not put them on the roofs. Still less do they place effigies of themselves drinking tea or smoking pipes of tobacco in company in front of their houses, and whether they ever planted palm-trees at regular intervals, in order later on, when they were sufficiently grown, to build roofs on their green stems and to erect dwelling-houses under them, is extremely doubtful. Here, however, the architect must be excused, since he had not a free hand, but had to follow a design drawn by the king; and generally speaking, the house would not have been sufficiently characteristic and distinct, had not these palm-trees and these effigies of Chinese amusing themselves under them introduced an obviously Chinese element, seeing that neither real palm-trees nor real Chinese were to be had."[82]   The wall of the circular room inside was to have been painted in Chinese style, but Büring, the architect, was behind-hand with his designs, and the king, being in a hurry, approved the scheme suggested by the sculptor Müller, with quantities of Chinese porcelain on a variety of consoles (Figure 12).

In Bruchsaal, in 1729, an 'Indian Garden-house' is mentioned, and the reference appears to be to a pavilion similar to that of Potsdam;[83] the garden-house was pulled down later, and so shared the fate of many of these creations of the mode; this explains how it comes that so few of them are now to be seen.

We may mention here as a curiosity the country-house of the Archbishop of Cologne. The Archbishop, Clemens August, who was fond of having himself carried through his diocese in a chair like a mandarin, also in his character of Rococo prince built several palaces, and among them Brühl. And as, after the time of Clemens Josef and after the Thirty Years' War, the Archbishopric of Cologne stood in close relationship with Bavaria, he took advantage of this connexion to obtain the services of the architect Girard, who for ten years had been successfully at work in Nymphenburg and Schleissheim, and had experience in *chinoiseries*. From the Chinese house at Brühl it is clear that since the *Trianon de porcelaine* and the 'Pagoda-tower,' something more had been learnt of Chinese architecture; the roofs showed concave curves, the whole building was long in plan and one-storeyed, the corners of the roof had small bells as ornamental pendants. '*Maison sans gêne*' it was called by the prince-bishop; a retreat in which, after the manner of Chinese dignitaries in their summer residences, one could take one's ease, free of all ceremony. Not far from the Chinese house there is also in Brühl a so-called 'Snail-house'—" something halfway between the old *Schneckenberg* (a hill with winding paths up it) and a Chinese tower."[84]

In interior architecture also certain Chinese influences can be established, at least as regards decorative motives. Along with the roof-form, was adopted a peculiar style of roof-window.   We are familiar with the elaborately-flourished framework of these windows from all sorts of Rococo buildings. The charming elaboration of such single features is perhaps to be connected with the predilection felt after the Regency, and under Chinese influence, for the architecture and decoration of framework generally. In the East, up to almost the end of the sixteenth century, a simple rectangular frame had been usual. It was only in the course of the seventeenth century that a richer style became established.[85] In the letter of 1743 already quoted, Attiret says: " I was constrained to come here in order to see doors and windows of every shape and form; round, oval, quadrangular, and polygonal; in the form of fans, flowers, vases, birds, beasts, fishes—in short, in all forms regular and irregular." Framework of this kind could naturally, as a rule, only be used for windows which had not to be opened—roof-windows, therefore, in particular. But the architects of the Rococo were in the habit of giving at least some adjunct of fantastic form even to doors and windows which had to be opened.[86] With these window and door frames, European architecture took over as well the Chinese latticework for balustrades and windows. It was first used freely in pavilions and garden-houses, and then became popular in furniture designs, notably Chippendale's (Figure 13 and Figure 14).

The builders of the European pleasure-house of the Rococo took from their Chinese models the habit of bringing the rooms into as close touch as possible with nature outside by means of high window-like openings reaching to the ground.[87]

Moreover, they disliked sharp angles and corners in their rooms. Even to these smallest details the spirit of the times penetrated and made its influence felt. Smooth-mannered men, flexible and supple, were the men of the Rococo, and their character expressed itself in every trifling production of their art. Thus the affinity which they felt for Chinese art led them to welcome the latest refinement of Chinese interior-architecture, the ' round corner,' if the expression is allowed. The bevelling of angles, which was first tried on plaster ceilings, soon led to the rounding off of all corners. Nothing perhaps, strange as it may appear, produced such revolutionary effects on the whole interior-architecture of the eighteenth century as this adoption of the ' Chinese corner.' The panels, which play so prominent

a part in the wall-covering of the Rococo, even the chests
and the cupboards and the profiles of the cornices, had to
have their angles rounded, in order not to injure the style.
The upper angles of door and window lintels, and even the
vertical corners of rooms, were not allowed to escape.[88]

Many examples from Germany might be given in illustration of this, but that is a task for a longer separate
treatise. We will only add here, by way of appendix, the
account of a singular plan, designed in Russia—the model
for the Smolni monastery in Petersburg, made in 1744, and
now in the Petersburg Academy of Arts. What first strikes
the eye is the gigantic tower over the entrance-gate, which
presents in its pagoda-like profile a curious mixture of
palladian and Chinese. One is reminded of the phrase used
by Le Comte in speaking of the gigantic pagodas, which in
China are planted on top of the great gates: " Great pavilions
in Gothic style."[89] That the plan for the Smolni monastery
really originated under Chinese influence is proved beyond
doubt by numerous angle-pavilions in Chinese style on the
huge surrounding wall. There is nothing surprising in that,
for Peter the Great had always taken pains to establish good
and useful relations with China. For instance, he brought
Chinese bridge-builders to Russia; for the fame of the Chinese
bridges was then general.*

Alongside of these practical influences of Far Eastern
architecture on the West, mention must also be made of a
case in which it had a like stimulating effect on European
art-theory. The *Sketch of an Historical Architecture*, by
Johann Gerhardt Fischer of Erlach, deserves to be recalled
to memory, since it has not received the attention it deserves.
Not that the sketch is either in content or form a complete
work. It was from this point of view as good or as bad
as the archæological knowledge of the author's times allowed.
At bottom, indeed, Fischer was a classicist, but we are
interested in him because he was the first professional art-
theorist to do full justice to the style of the Far East.
Previous histories of art had only concerned themselves
with the European antique and with post-Renaissance art.
It is remarkable, however, that Fischer also passes over
Gothic art without showing any understanding of it; in

* " In Europe there are no such bold bridges as there are in China."[90]

a single passage of his introduction he does no more than refer to it slightingly as ' *Schnörkelwerk* '*;* in the spirit of his time he looked upon Gothic as an aberration. The more remarkable is it that he freely included in his purview the Asiatic styles. For the first time it is recognized that really scientific art-history is only possible on the basis of a comparison of all the phenomena, of all the styles. In the Dedication he says, " wherein every people must be allowed its own way of thinking no less than its own taste." The book was intended for ' Amateurs and Artists.' For that reason only such achievements could be noticed as seemed adapted " to provide artists with a stimulus to invention." For his section on China, Fischer had studied the *Novus Atlas Sinensis* of Martinus Martini and Neuhof's report on the mission of the East Indian Company to China. He gives illustrations of Chinese bridges, of the city of Peking, of the Porcelain tower of Nanking, of the pagodas, of the artificial caves; not even the Chinese pleasure-mountains are forgotten.[91] The work was translated into English in 1730. It is quite possible that this translation was of use to the English architect, Chambers, who later paid a professional visit to China, and so to his (in its time) celebrated work on Chinese architecture. Of this we shall have more to say presently.

As one briefly reviews all these Rococo *chinoiseries*—in the style of dress, in porcelain-decoration of rooms, in lacquer furniture, in the exterior and interior of buildings—the idea is forced upon one that social life also must have borrowed something here and there from China.

First there were the shadow plays, which were first naturalized in Germany and passed from there to France, where, after 1767, they were known as ' *ombres chinoises.*'[92] At first they were only given in certain *salons*, but soon became a popular entertainment.

In Paris, as the centre of fashion, there came, in the course of time, to be quite a number of social resorts, which were known as ' Chinese.' There was a ' Chinese Café,' where the service was done by two women in Chinese costume, and where a real Chinese porter received the guests and showed them out. There is a certain bitter humour in the fact that it was this place which served as headquarters to Gaius

Gracchus Babeuf and his friends. A second ' Chinese Café '
is mentioned only. A ' *Redoute chinoise* ' was opened in 1781
in the Faubourg Saint Laurent, in which Chinese pageants
and Chinese illuminations were to be seen, also Chinese
fireworks, which were then quite common. One of the
popular Chinese swings was served by a Chinese man and
a Chinese woman. A ' *Jeu de bagne chinois*,' perhaps a fore-
runner of the modern Merry-go-round, was also among the
amusements of the place.

The Chinese baths, with their Chinese, Turkish, and
Persian architecture, inspired Cuisin to write the following
lines dedicated ' To the Chinese, formerly called the Oriental,
baths, situated in the Boulevard italien ':

> " *Quel pays merveilleux ! Sans sortir de Paris,*
> *Dans le Palais-Royal, vous avez des Chinoises :*
> *Un orchestre chinois, arrivé de Pékin,*
> *Exécute, en ronflant, un solo de Martin :*
> *Mais dans les Bains chinois c'est un autre artifice.*
> *D'un kiosque élégant tracez-vous l'édifice.*
> *Sous des rochers de plâtre en amas rocailleux*
> *D'une grotte en carton à l'aspect gracieux.*
> *Ainsi le Parisien, tout près de sa maison*
> *Peut, la canne à la main, aborder à Canton.*"[93]

Outside in the Parks, too, China provided colour and
interest; in the midst of pavilions and grottoes the earliest
pheasant-houses gleamed with the golden plumage of their
Oriental denizens, while under Chinese bridges sported the
first gold-fish, that rare species, the production of which had
cost the Chinese perhaps a thousand years of patient care,
and which now, since La Pompadour had received the first
specimens as a present, were becoming known in Europe.[94]

And it was quite of a piece with this bizarre, exotic notion
which people had of China, that they should have taken it
as the motive of their burlesque entertainments. In Paris
and Vienna to begin with, and later in other courts, balls
and masquerades in Chinese costume were held; and these
amusements became, in the course of the century, so much
the fashion, that at last the whole people came to engage
in them. Even the pupils of the *Académie de France* in
Rome were not to be deprived of their Chinese masquerade.
In Paris these amusements soon spread to the Fairs and to
the Boulevards, where Chinese *Redoutes* were built, and

where the '*Théâtre des récréations de la Chine* ' arose.[95] Chinese jokes even invaded light opera and comedy. The small theatres in particular took them up, and the Italian Comedians especially. In 1692, this company played for the first time, in the presence of the king in the Hôtel Bourgogne, the five-act comedy of Regnard and Dufresny, *Les Chinois*. The Harlequin of this farce gave himself out as a ' Chinese doctor,' and the scene was laid in a Chinese cabinet.[96]

In 1723, Nestier's troupe gave in the Faubourg Saint Germain *Arlequin, Barbet, Pagode et Médecin*, a Chinese piece in two Acts. The scene represented the outside of the Imperial Palace at Peking. At the end of this extravaganza the ' King of China ' pardons his children in the oracular French-Chinese phrase—" Pardonaon, levaon, divertissaon, dansaon." They obey and dance, and the curtain falls.[97]

In 1729, the same players gave in Saint Laurent *La Princesse de la Chine*.[98] The scene is again laid in Peking. But the *dramatis personæ* must have presented an extra-ordinary medley of types from every part of Asia. Among them we have: the King of China, the Princess Diamantine, the Prince of Basta, the Prince Nureddin, the Heir Apparent of Wisapur, the inevitable Colas, whose figure—he was supposed to have been Secretary of State in early China—is a reminiscence of the missionaries' letters.

In connexion with the presence of some Chinese visitors in Paris, originated two charming little plays, the characters in which, returning from France to their home in China, proclaim their love for France.[99] One of these returned travellers cleverly convinces the daughter of a Mandarin that France is the most wonderful country in the world, on the ground, flattering for a French, though not for a Chinese, lady, that there the ladies of Paris govern the men, whereas in China it is the other way round.

The list of such pieces might run to almost any length. In the eighteenth century the East exercised an influence which it would be difficult to overrate on the initial develop-ment of the lyrical stage—the later Opera. No great works resulted, but the simple, unpretentious musical comedies, in contrast with the severe style of classical tragedy, which had almost monopolized the stage of the seventeenth century, educated a taste for variety, and opened up the stage to the sentimental imagination which till then had only found vent in the novel.

These ' picturesque ' Chinese romances, which a touch of satire often only made more piquant, were fairly numerous. The satire was prompted by the success of the *Lettres persanes* of Montesquieu. Among the twenty successors of these letters—Turkish, Indian, Siamese, Peruvian, Muscovite, Roumanian, Judean, Iroquois—which appeared in the course of the century, were several collections of Chinese letters: for example, the *Lettres chinoises* of the Marquis d'Argens, a name behind which the French Sinologist, Henri Cordier, wrongly discovers Frederick the Great as the real author; or the *Lettres chinoises, indiennes et tartares par un Bénédictin*, the true inventor of which, Voltaire, dedicated them to a student of China, his friend Pauw at the court of Frederick the Great. Among these satires belongs also the *Espion chinois en Europe* of Cassagne, a similar work by Grudar, the mere title of which betrays its exciting contents: *L'espion chinois ou l'Envoyé secret de la Cour de Pékin pour examiner l'État de l'Europe. Traduit du chinois;* also the *Relation de Phihihu, émissaire de l'Empereur de la Chine en Europe.* All these were really only second or third rate ' literature,' but their mass vouches for the wide popularity of this Chinese matter. The ' letters ' often appeared in the form of a newsletter; for example, the ' Chinese letters ' of the Marquis d'Argens came out every Monday and Thursday in a series of little brochures of eight pages, and when d'Argens broke off after the hundred and fiftieth number, it was only because he fell ill. At the close, the letters became merely a compilation from the wide reading of the author, developed his utopias and projects of reform, or attacked his enemies.

This little excursion into literature may perhaps seem out of place, but in truth all these things are equally of value as witnesses to a state of feeling, which impressed itself on everything, from the façades of palaces to the intimate enjoyments of personal life, whether these took the form of fantastic thought or expressed themselves in the fanciful curves of furniture. For the question of style, it makes no difference whether we tell of a passing rage for Chinese pageantry or recall a saying of Grimm of November, 1785, that at a certain date 'most of our furniture' was 'made in the Chinese taste.' Everywhere the same style was alive. How it developed can only be shown by accumulating examples; and so we may conclude our studies of the Rococo with some account of its development in furniture. The transformation of the style from Baroque to Rococo had its origin in the Royal Manufactory of Furniture in Paris. At the French court, there was already at the beginning of the seventeenth century a quantity of Chinese furniture, of lacquer-work in particular. A knowledge of it has been made accessible by a modern work[100] based on the *Inventaire Général du Mobilier de la Couronne*, the *Inventaire du Versailles*, the *Inventaire des meubles du Château de Versailles* of 1708, and the *Journal du Garde-Meuble de la Couronne* of 1666–1672. According to this, Mazarin had already collected such things as curiosities; at any rate, Madame de Montpensier speaks in her Memoirs under the year 1658 of Chinese furniture in her possession. The Dauphin, an admirer of Oriental art, had his apartments provided with Chinese furniture at an equally early date. In 1689 the king's eldest brother arranged a lottery, in which Chinese furniture was among the prizes. Madame de Maintenon also had Chinese furniture at Versailles and Trianon. In the Trianon, '*ameublement à la chinoise*' was already the phrase used. This would indicate that at that time, in the second half of the seventeenth century, Chinese furniture was already being imitated. It was some decades before the new form, modified to suit European requirements, came into general use. Even in his day Bérain had to adapt himself to the new curves in his designs for furniture. The Chinese lacquers served as models; the transition was formed by the copied lacquer furniture of Langlois and Essarts, and the new form became generally established in the furniture of the Rococo. As in architectural ornament, and decoration generally, so here it was the vigorous, free curve which won its way; and here again models were provided by the Chinese (Figure 15).

We cannot, indeed, bring ourselves to agree with Laske's far too sweeping view,[101] when he thinks it may be "confidently asserted that without the strong influence of

Japanese and Chinese craftsmanship there would have
been no Baroque and no Rococo art in France, and, therefore, none in the rest of Europe." The thing cannot be
stated in such downright terms. Assuredly China played
a considerable part in the development of style in the Rococo,
but a looser style of a similar character would have arisen
even without this influence. ' Rococo ' was too deeply
rooted in the whole moral and social composition of the
Europe of those days.

How such phenomena are engendered from the most
intimate intellectual, or rather spiritual, conditions, a
comparison may make clear. In the eighties of the nineteenth century, the appearance was noted of an ' English
Rococo ' as a curious temporary phase of culture. This
development is generally known among theorists of art as
' English æstheticism.' The fact that Botticelli, although
he had been known long before, has since then continued to
be a special favourite with the English public, is to be
ultimately ascribed to a state of soul which once more preferred just these lines and just these colours rather than
others. That Rossetti was admired at the time along with
Botticelli, that his favourite flowers, the lily, with its soft
delicate curves and slender stem, and the sunflower, were
to be seen on so many tables in England—who can say why
this was so ? All that can be said is that people did fall in
love once more with the delicate colours and graceful stems
of these flowers; they fell in love, too, with the delicate
hues of porcelain. Rossetti collected blue and white
Chinese porcelain. And all England, by unuttered mutual
consent, suddenly did the same. Need it then astonish us
to learn that the old eighteenth-century furniture was once
more dragged forth from dusty lumber-rooms, just for the
sake of its delicately curved lines ? Chairs, wardrobes, and
elegant spider-legged tables again received the place of
honour. For the furniture of Sheraton, so long dispos-
sessed by the plain and solid Victorian furniture, every
village and every cottage was ransacked. Even the furniture factories remodelled themselves on Chippendale and
Sheraton.[102] It was the ' lovesick ' tenderness of Rossetti's
life which gave to the whole artistic expression of these few
years, this St Martin's summer, its distinctive note.

Was the case otherwise with the Rococo of the eighteenth century ? In external circumstance, certainly, but not in inner significance. Men's feeling for a particular form is only an expression of their whole being. Men possessed of artistic faculties, unless they are entirely independent and forceful characters, seek to find somewhere the complete embodiment of that feeling for form which is germinant within themselves. The Rococo of the eighteenth century thought it had found this perfection in China; the short-lived English Rococo of the nineteenth century needed only to look back a hundred and fifty years in its own history to see its clarified image in the glass.

THE ENLIGHTENMENT

THE ENLIGHTENMENT

WHEN we speak here of 'Rococo' or 'Enlightenment,' we understand by the terms the expression taken by certain spiritual phenomena which—and we are dealing here with quite unique occurrences—succeeded in finding a form correspondent to their 'idea.' The word 'Rococo' conjures up for all our senses a world of subtle charm and loveliness; we hear the skipping airs of the first operettas, and mingling with them the rustle of splendid silken robes. We seem to scent in the air the fine fragrance of powdered wigs, to see the correct and yet mobile figures of a brilliant society moving in step to the air of a Mozart minuet, to be dazzled by the countless lights reflected from the mirror-covered walls and the lacquered cabinets of spacious saloons, we are enchanted by the indescribable wealth of colour of a world splendid with silk and porcelain. We feel clearly that in all this an unique feeling for life has found its unique form of expression, that here 'idea' has become form, irradiating even all external things with the mysterious light of its essence. We see this world as a separate whole, whose unity is in no way impaired by the fact that other worlds with other actualities maintain a parallel existence—the hard struggle for life of the oppressed peasantry, excluded from the enjoyment of this brilliant world, bloody war, the self-denying labours of the man of science—all these worlds had their separate existences, because each had its own separate laws. To take an almost grotesque example—during the War of the Spanish Succession, the export of Paris mannequins (fashion-dolls) for the benefit of the *beau monde* of Vienna went on without interruption !

With the Enlightenment, we feel ourselves transported not into the perfumed and vibrant atmosphere of the *salon*, but into the cool, severe air of the study. Never has ' pure thought' exercised so fascinating a power over men as at the height of the Rococo, in the fourth and fifth decades of the eighteenth century. 'Enlightenment' signifies for us the world of constructive thought. The soul of it is Mathematics (Mathematics of the Kosmos—Leibniz; Mathematics of the Human Mind—La Mettrie; Mathematics of Industry—Quesnay); all expressions of the same intellectual attitude, bent on regarding its objects in the light of a preconceived principle. But, while the Rococo was song or poetry feeling, the Enlightenment was computation with thoughts. 'Rococo' and 'Enlightenment' are accordingly essentially opposed, because they are developments of opposed 'ideas.' Here also extremes meet.

And these very opposites we find curiously united in the Chinese world—the yearning for the universal, that knows of no limits, no law; and the rational thinking, that seeks for a fixed standpoint, and uses laws as guide-lines for its cautious, critical procedure; intuition and science incorporated in the two greatest men in Chinese history: Lao Tzŭ and Kung Fu-tzŭ.

The Rococo was essentially the negation of law. Like the spray from a fountain, the snowy plaster-ornamentations are splashed on walls and ceilings; the Rococo has recorded its love for moving water in countless artificial water-works. The clothes of the period were bespangled with random flower-forms; brush and chisel, in obedience to Briseux' precept, vied with one another in imitating ' Nature '—' Nature ' who produces her infinite variety of forms without repetition and apparently without law. This is the same spirit in which Kung once said of Lao Tzŭ:

> " He orders nought,
> And yet is nought confounded."

In Lao Tzŭ's personality, the soul of the Rococo touches the soul of the Far East. The art which produced the delicate porcelains and the flowery silks of Fu-kien went back in spirit to Lao Tzŭ. In the lacquer cabinets and the porcelain, in the vaporous colouring of the silks, in all the precious things which Europe welcomed as ' *la Chine*,' it was the soul of Lao Tzŭ which spoke.

The Enlightenment, on the contrary, was Thought obeying laws. It was the effort of the intellect, after its schooling in the exact sciences of the seventeenth century, to build up,

with the help of its one unfailing instrument, the concept
of causality, a new ' rational ' world, to open the door to
a ' rational ' world-order. Thus arose a state of tension
between the thinking Ego and the world of Being, between
what should be and what is—even between the present and
history, since, in the extreme twilight of the past, men fancied
they could discern a reflexion of that which their desires
projected upon the future. And it is no mere accident that,
while the philosophers of the Enlightenment were much
occupied with the condition of human society and the
structure of the state, Confucius, likewise, had devoted his
attention principally to civic life.

The organs of knowledge were highly esteemed, while the
emotional faculties of the soul and the poetic imagination
were pushed into the background. There was a return to
the stoic principle, which based virtue on right knowledge.
Thus, a practical interest in human affairs at last removed
even ethics into the sphere of abstract reasoning. Men
freed themselves from the limitations imposed by theology
and scholastic metaphysics, and rose above the half-mytho-
logical, speculative, natural philosophy of the Renaissance,
to follow the laws implicit in the nature of things itself.

In accordance with a practical humanitarian ideal, they
sought to reconcile culture and religion, and took into their
service the morality (but not the dogmas) of Christianity.
This cultural ideal had for ethical basis only ' virtue ';
positive religion was almost completely discarded. Then
came the first translations of Confucius and the Chinese
classics; and men discovered, to their astonishment, that
more than two thousand years ago in China, whose name
was already on the tongue of every salesman at the great
fairs, Confucius had thought the same thoughts in the same
manner, and fought the same battles. They read in his book
the words: " If a man make himself understood by his
speech, the end is attained." He, too, then had advocated
clearness in verbal expression and, therefore, also clearness
of logical thought generally. Thus Confucius became the
patron saint of eighteenth-century Enlightenment. Only
through him could it find a connecting link with China.
Only Confucius and the classical books were translated and
read. Lao Tzŭ might equally well have been translated,

but this was only done at a later time. What could the Enlightenment expect to get from a sage who chose "to talk to men in parables "? who had uttered the mystic saying: "Only with one who understands the meaning of words can one speak without words "? The Enlightenment knew only the China of Confucius. The study of his classical works gave a decisive impulsion to the development of the history of religion. It is remarkable to observe how, in the course of the eighteenth century, three names unite to form a triple constellation—Mohammed, Confucius, Zoroaster. Mohammed had already been discovered by Europe through the active Turkish studies of the seventeenth century—a result of the great Turkish wars.[1] Then, during the whole first half of the eighteenth century, Confucius was the one centre of interest, and it was only in, or about, 1770 that Zoroaster was discovered.* And, as if to close this chapter of shifting predilections, de Pastoret fused the legendary accounts of the three founders of Asiatic religions into one work: *Zoroastre, Confuzius et Mahomet.*

In the first decades of the eighteenth century the Enlightenment-work of the Jesuits on China bore rich fruit. " In the last century we hardly knew of China," says Voltaire in the *Essai sur les mœurs* (chapter ii). As early as 1735, Du Halde is able to announce in his famous book that the bulk of the work has been accomplished,[2] and in 1769, it was actually stated in print that " China is better known than some provinces of Europe itself."[3] During these years the Jesuit mission never wearied of heaping benedictions, as one of the Fathers says, " on a government which has brought such wise laws into being."[4] It was possible for Bossuet in a treatise on world-history, to omit all mention of the Far East, without drawing down upon himself the reproaches of his contemporaries; a century later his omission incurred the censure of Voltaire.

The year 1700 was, even for literature, the year of transition in which the affections of the learned world were turned towards China. " From this moment onwards, a

* The real discovery of Zoroaster was brought about by Anquetil du Perron's translation of the Zend-Avesta, 1771. We must not omit to remark that the strongest stimulus to the comparative history of religion came from Islam. Confucius was regarded rather as a moral teacher than as the founder of a religion.

clear conviction banished all uncertainty, and every one was forced to admire a people as old as it is wise, and as pre-eminent in religion as in wisdom," says a contemporary.[5]

With Voltaire's *Essai sur les mœurs* of the year 1760 admiration of China reached its zenith. The book is a perfect compendium of all the feelings of the time about the Far East.

Meanwhile we must return to the first points of contact established between the philosophers of the Enlightenment and classical Chinese philosophy. Leibniz was the first to recognize the great intellectual importance of Chinese culture for the development of the West. His doctrine of Monads coincides curiously in many points with Chinese ideas about ' the universal,' as they are expressed in the three great exponents of Chinese life, in Lao Tzŭ, in Confucius, and in the Chinese form of Buddhism. The doctrine of a ' pre-established harmony ' has its Chinese counterpart in the *Tao of the world*. Leibniz believes, like the Chinese sages, in the world of reality as a unity, as a continuously rising scale of spiritual beings developing progressively. In the one case as in the other, from the belief in pre-established harmony as from belief in the Tao of the world, an unlimited optimism resulted. (' The best of all possible worlds '—' The Kingdom of Heaven.') For Leibniz, as for Confucius, the kernel of all religion, the Christian religion included, lies in practical life. Their essential service is, in his view, the creation of knowledge, their end education for socially useful action. This is the plain and simple gospel of the whole Enlightenment. It is quite in the sense of Confucius' saying: " Knowledge of the *Tao* leads to Virtue."' And in the one case as in the other Virtue signifies Happiness (*Glück-seligkeit*), that is, to the supreme end of all thought.

Leibniz had quite early occupied himself with Chinese philosophy. Clearly, the first works that came into his hands were Kircher's *China monumentis illustrata* (1667), and the *De re literaria Sinensium* of Th. Spicelius (1660);[6] already in 1669, he concludes his sketch of *Suggestions for the institution in Germany of an Academy or Society for the encouragement of Arts and Sciences* with a glance at China. In 1679, he was taking a lively interest in the publication projected by Provost Andreas Müller of Berlin of a *Clavis*

Sinica,[7] and his letters on the subject raise a number of questions which show that he already knew a great deal about China. In 1687, in a letter to the Landgrave Ernst of Hessen-Rheinfels, he mentions " the work of Confucius, the king of Chinese philosophers, which has been published this year in Paris,"[8] and makes it clear that he has read the book carefully.[9]

In 1689, during his visit to Rome, Leibniz was able to make the acquaintance of the Jesuit, Père Grimaldi, who had long been working in China and who was soon to return thither. An active correspondence between Leibniz and Grimaldi followed, to which the former was indebted for the best of his knowledge of China.

All this knowledge, with the expectations and hopes that arose from it, took form in the introduction to the *Novissima Sinica*, which Leibniz published in 1697. Here he develops the boldest and most far-reaching schemes.

In the *præfatio* he ascribes to a special dispensation of Providence the fact that from the two ends of the earth, Europe and China, two great civilizations had at that particular epoch met, and fertilized one another. And he has no doubt that Providence further designs to draw the intervening countries also (*e.g.*, Russia) into the circle of this great civilization. He says that the West certainly surpasses the East in the theoretic and philosophical sciences (Mathematics, Astronomy, Logic, Metaphysic); but, on the other hand, China is undoubtedly superior to us in practical philosophy, in political morality. It was astonishing, what beneficent effects the rules of Confucius had had on the ordering of private and public life.[10] Without the gracious intervention of Heaven, such virtue in the Chinese was inexplicable. How much might not Europe, so highly developed in the theoretic sciences, learn in these matters of practical life from the Chinese. Then he goes on: " The condition of affairs among ourselves seems to me to be such that, in view of the inordinate lengths to which the corruption of morals has advanced, I almost think it necessary that Chinese missionaries should be sent to us to teach us the aim and practice of natural theology, as we send missionaries to them to instruct them in revealed theology. For I believe that if a wise man were to be appointed judge—not of the beauty of goddesses, but of the goodness of peoples—he would award the golden apple to the Chinese—unless, indeed, we should outdo them in nobility by conferring on them that which is, indeed, a superhuman good—the divine gift of the Christian religion.

But Leibniz was not a man to be content with mere reflexions: he was always eager to realize his ideas. As he himself once put it: " True Faith and true Hope is not only to speak and not only to think, but to speak *practice*—that is, to act as if the truth were so."[11]   Accordingly he had already, in his various suggestions for the founding of a Society, spoken repeatedly of the " organization of all practical scientific work, and the enlistment of all the intellectual forces in the service of productive activity." We need only mention in this connexion his plan for a universal language and for a reunion of the Churches.

Nor did he desire his *Novissima Sinica* to be regarded as a mere scientific treatise, but as an appeal to the Protestant world to join hands with the Catholic in establishing contact with the East.

But Leibniz went far beyond this. He laboured unwearyingly at all the preliminaries for his Oriental schemes. He worked hard for the foundation of the Berlin Society of Sciences, and this simply in order to have an active instrument for the " Opening up of China and the interchange of civilizations between China and Europe."[12]   At the same time, he promoted the foundation of a similar society in Moscow, which was to be a link between Western Europe and China. He hoped in this way to open for Prussia, by means of its good relations with Peter the First, the landroute to China.[13]

At the instance of Leibniz, Jablonski in 1700 presented a " most humble suggestion for the institution of *Observatorii et Academiæ Scientiarum* in the capital of Churbrandenburg." In the petition stress is laid on " the example of France, England, and China."[14]   The Electress Sophia was not well disposed to all these distant schemes, and remarked scornfully that " the greatness of the ruler of Brandenburg would no doubt not be complete until, like the kings of India, he had an astrologer always at his elbow."[15]

In the general instruction drafted for the members of Leibniz' Society in the year 1700 we read: " We will make it our business, in addition to the promotion of trade and serviceable relations with our friend, the Czar, to see that useful *observationes astronomicæ geograficæ*, and also *nationum, linguarum et morum rerumque artificialium et naturalium et nobis incognitarum*,[16] and the like, shall be made and sent in to the Society."

It is strange to find Leibniz propounding in this connexion the idea of controlling and limiting book-production by means of a commission appointed by the State. It is very possible that he borrowed it from China.

At the end of his residence in Berlin Leibniz drew up in a memorandum for the king a list of the services rendered by the Society since its foundation; here among other items we find the following: " certain very ancient symbols of the Chinese have been elucidated, which for two thousand years past they have themselves been unable to understand, and which nevertheless contain a new mathematical key."[17] Leibniz here alludes to one of his pet ideas, his *Ars combinatoria*.[18] He attributed quite peculiar value to this art. By its help he believed that he could, with a few figures, prove the creation of the 'All' out of the 'Nothing.'[19] In 1697, he wrote to Duke Rudolf August of Wolfenbüttel: " For one of the principal articles of the Christian faith, and one of those which have been least examined by lay philosophers, . . . is the creation of things from nothing by the almighty power of God. Now it may be said with confidence that nothing in the world gives a better idea of this creation, nay almost a demonstration of it, than the origin of numbers, as herein described . . . and it will scarcely be possible to find in nature and philosophy a better image of this mystery." Leibniz knew that this binary arithmetic of his was related to the hexagrams of I-ching,[20] and from the combination of the two he looked for help in the missionary work to be conducted in China.[21] In 1697, he wrote on the subject to the Jesuit Verjus: " This new philosophical counting, since it is common to all languages, will give even the remotest peoples, whose speech differs so widely from our own, such as the Chinese, an idea of the most important and highest truths of natural religion."[22]

And in similar terms he wrote to the Duke of Wolfenbüttel in 1697:[23] "Thus I thought well to communicate to him (*i.e.*, to Père Grimaldi in China) this conception of numbers, in the hope, since he tells me himself[24] that the monarch of this mighty empire is much addicted to the art of computation, and learnt the European manner of counting from Grimaldi's predecessor, Father Verbiest, that possibly this image of the mystery of creation might enable him to discern more and more clearly the excellence of the Christian faith."

For reasons into which we cannot go, Leibniz was obliged to give up his work on the Society. When, in 1706, a letter from Moscow provided the opportunity of establishing relations with Asia, it was not utilized; for Leibniz, the moving spirit, was no longer on the spot.

One at least of his preliminary labours eventually bore fruit: on March 28, 1707, the Society was granted the privilege of growing mulberries for silk-worm culture.[25] Moreover, as a result of Leibniz' activity the Society, in 1710, published in Vol. I of *Miscellanea Berolinensia* an essay by La Groze: *De libris Sinensium Bibl. reg. Berolinensis*.[26]

More important was the personal influence which Leibniz had on A. H. Francke and Christian Wolff. Francke took charge of the political and missionary side of his schemes, while Wolff quite plainly and unmistakably placed philosophy on the same footing with the Confucian conception of the world.[27]

A. H. Francke received the *Novissima Sinica* with enthusiasm. Soon after its appearance, he wrote to Leibniz (July 9, 1697): "The *Novissima Sinica* which you have published and the introduction thereto, so excellent and so perfect in form, induce me to send you my personal thanks for this magnificent work."[28] Thus began an epistolary discussion of these problems between Leibniz and Francke which went on until 1714.

As has been already remarked, Francke gained from this only a missionary interest in China. He did not see so far as Leibniz, who attributed to these relations between West and East enormous importance as agencies for the unification of the world.[29] Francke's position is well indicated by a paper ascribed to him by his biographer, G. Kramer.[30]

It is preserved at Halle in the *Archiv* of the Francke foundation. *Pharus missionis evangelicæ, seu consilium de propa-
ganda fide per conversionem ethnicorum maxime Sinesium
prodomus fusioris operis ad potentissimum regem Prussiæ
Fridericum.* The paper, it is true, was neither printed nor
laid before the Society. It obviously dates from the time
of the founding of the *Collegii orientalis theologici.* This
college, founded in 1707 by Francke in Halle, was intended
to be a school for missionaries, in the curriculum of which
' Sinic ' should be included. But these philological aims
found little sympathy in Germany. The leading German
Sinologists of the eighteenth century sought a field for them-
selves abroad, since their native land failed to recognize
the importance of their work. Klaproth took service at the
Russian court, Mohl went to France, Neumann to England.
Even at the end of the century, Chinese studies are only
pursued as a hobby. Wilhelm von Humboldt studied
Chinese for the sake of his work on the history of language;
Goethe and Rückert came into momentary contact with the
Chinese language when they discovered the beauty of
Chinese poetry.

From the same town of Halle, in which Francke had
founded his *Collegium orientale theologicum*, Christian Wolff
was later obliged to take flight on account of a lecture on
Chinese philosophy. On retiring from the position of Pro-
rector in favour of Lange, the professor of Theology, Wolff,
on July 12, 1721, gave an address *de Sinarum Philosophia
Practica.*[31] On account of this address he was accused
before the king of atheism, and there followed the notorious
Royal command directing Wolff to leave Halle and the
kingdom immediately. The University of Marburg had the
courage to offer a refuge to the expelled professor. Later,
Frederick the Great recalled him to Prussia.

In his address, Wolff sought an understanding in two
directions. On the one hand he avows his agreement with
the ancient wisdom of China, on the other he adheres to the
Christian faith, as if the two were fundamentally the same
thing. He attempts to show that the moral doctrine of
Confucius in no way conflicts with Christian morality, and
that it is, nevertheless, in complete agreement with natural
morality. From such a position conclusions certainly followed

which could not but appear highly dangerous to the theological faculty of Halle in those days.

"Whatever it is," says Wolff, "that moves a man to action, whether revealed truths or such as are established by natural phenomena, he will, whether he be Christian or Confucian, act virtuously." There is according to Wolff a 'Lydian stone' by which every action must be tested. It must not run counter to the nature of the human spirit. From this point of view, Chinese virtues and customs had brilliantly justified themselves, since they were found without exception to be in harmony with the human spirit.

Such opinions were not uncommon at that time within the circle of Catholic theology. The majority of Jesuits had long since supported the view that the followers of Confucius believed in the same god as the Christians. And the headquarters of Catholic theology, the University of Paris, was then the centre of the enthusiasm for China. There, the Jesuits saw to it that these problems were unceasingly discussed. Indeed, it may safely be said that occupation with these questions was largely instrumental in forcing the theological faculty of Paris in the direction of Deism. We possess a treatise which shows that this movement was clearly perceived by the adherents of the old theology.[32] It is obvious that the writer's student-days lay thirty-five years back, at the beginning of the century. He feels lost among the new problems. Language, method, problems—all is new to him. "To what purpose all these questions about the Mosaic chronology, which they compare with the fabulous Chinese methods of time-reckoning, assigning by preference special importance to these latter, if it be not to awaken doubts about the authority of Holy Scripture, the foundation-stone of our religion?" The theological faculty of Paris seemed to him to be completely entangled in Molinism. It knew no middle way between Molinism and Jansenism, but drew its conclusions from the former, although with a certain caution.[33] But Deism and Natural Religion were the natural consequence of Molinism. This treatise shows that the discussions of the Sorbonne came very near to what Wolff had said in his address. The Catholic faculty in Paris showed itself to be less limited, and bolder in its thinking than the Protestant faculty of Halle.

Wolff's address, apart from its interest as a document of religious history, has a special merit. It contained the first full appreciation of Chinese scholasticism based on Noël's edition of the Chinese classics.[34] Wolff took his stand on the genuinely ' enlightened ' principle, on which ancient China had likewise acted, that knowledge of virtue leads of itself to virtuous action. (" Virtues and Vices cannot both have one dwelling-place.") Hence follows, as the first duty of the State, the teaching of virtue in schools. From this point of view, Wolff found the Chinese schools exemplary.

As similar principles have been discussed in later pedagogic literature, it is worth while to consider them briefly. Wolff recurs to the division of the school into an upper and a lower department, which he had discussed at length in his *Philosophia practica*. He says that no one before himself had understood the value of this division so well as the Chinese.[35] Thus in her best days China had the double school (*Schola parvulorum* and *schola adultorum*).[36] The *Schola parvulorum* comprised all children between the ages of eight and fifteen.[37] As children of this age are not yet capable of reasoning (*ratio*), the lower school only trained the senses (*sensus*). It still appealed to fear of the superior part of the soul, the conscience. The upper school afterwards taught self-government through the power of the superior part of the soul, whose *ratio* acted as a guide to virtuous action.* The upper school was only attended by a selection of the most gifted pupils. It gave a training in the government of self and of others. For as not all *intelligentes* can be rulers, the intelligence must be trained to service through self-discipline.[38]

To Wolff this seems the ideal education, because it follows the natural laws of the human spirit. Apart from this he approves the system because, according to it, the *ratio* in all its activities is connected with a definite end. Nothing is to be studied that has not Wisdom—*i.e.*, Happiness (*felicitas*)—for its aim.[39]

The Physiocrats, at a later time—we shall speak of them more fully presently—who honoured Wolff as a martyr alongside of Confucius and Christ, were certainly acquainted with this laudatory account of the old Chinese schools, and

---

* *Quomodo unusquisque se ipsum regere debeat, ut sponte faciat quod laudem meretur*, p. 68.

were confirmed by it in their most important contention—
viz., that only such a school-system could guide the people
into the right path and keep them in it. It would be interesting to discover whether, through the school of the
Physiocrats, it would be possible to trace back to Chinese
models the first schemes for State schools devised by Turgot
in his Ministry, and later by Condorcet, during the Revolution
—schemes which were, of course, never realized.

In justice to Wolff, it must be said that, as he makes clear
in his address, he had arrived independently at his own
philosophical position before the work of the Jesuit Noël
(1711) first made him acquainted with Chinese philosophy.
His own philosophy prepared him for the understanding of
the Confucian, and he found that Noël's commentary did
not do justice to the text. Even before the publication of
the Halle address, Wolff's pupil and colleague, Bülffinger
of Tübingen, was engaged upon a new presentation of Chinese
philosophy under the title *Specimen Doctrinæ Veterum
Sinarum Moralis et Politicæ; Tanquam Exemplum Philosophiæ Gentium ad Rem Publicam Applicatæ: Excerptum
Libellis Sinicæ Genti Classicis, Confucii sive Dicta, sive
Facta Complexis.*[40]

Bülffinger remarks in his dedication of the work to his
sovereign that it is an unusual thing to see a philosophical
work dedicated to the ruler of a State. But he hopes, in
view of the prince's love for the sciences, that he may be
stirred by this work to bring together again, even in European
territories, the two long-severed sisters, State-craft and
Philosophy.

Bülffinger also admired above all in China the union of
Politics and Morality; he saw in China—as did almost all the
' Enlighteners' of his time—the enviable country in which
kings were really philosophers.

*   *   *   *   *

It is curious to observe, as an example of the irony of
History, the fact that it was the Jesuits themselves, the
intermediaries *par excellence* between the Enlightenment
of ancient China and that of the eighteenth century, who
placed in the hands of Voltaire and the other Encyclopædists
the weapons which were one day to be turned against them-

selves. Voltaire, the most dangerous enemy of the Jesuits throughout the whole century, was educated in a Jesuit college, and gained there his first knowledge of China. The Brothers talked with admiration of the religion of the Mandarins, and with contempt of the superstition of the Bonzes. Voltaire gathered here the information which he later used in his attacks on those Fathers who now opened their minds to him so frankly and unsuspectingly.[41]

And what a friend to the Enlightenment Père Noël shows himself when he says in the preface to his edition of the six Chinese classics: "This Latin translation of the six classical books I present to you, dear reader, not only that you may become acquainted with what the Chinese have written, but that you may put into act what they have rightly thought."[42] The preface closes with the words: "*dum leges Sinarum doctrinam, Christianorum vitam cogita. Utinam utrisque lapis angularis fiat Christus.*"[43] And in another passage in the *Lettres édifiantes et curieuses*—we find the erroneous, but for the age of *Jus Naturæ* characteristic, opinion stated that in the Chinese classics were contained "the principles of natural law, which the ancient Chinese had received from the children of Noah."[44] The Jesuits were not even afraid to put popular abridgements of this dangerous doctrine into the hands of unlearned folk. The celebrated work *Confucius Sinarum Philosophus* (1687) was followed up by two simply written compendiums.[45] In the latter of the two it is boldly stated that Chinese morality is drawn "from the purest sources of natural reason." Of particular importance were the details given by the Jesuit Fathers concerning practical political matters in the Chinese Empire. On the one hand they helped forward the advocacy of enlightened despotism by philosophy, while on the other they gave a backbone to the physiocratic movement—that movement which, in anticipation of the Revolution, attempted to bolster up once more—this time from the economic side—the Absolutism of the seventeenth century. Here, in the domain of political theory, as in almost all the departments of science, China became the corner-stone of debate, a disturbing phantom in an age already sufficiently agitated.

A more or less generally accepted conception of the Chinese

had gradually formed itself in the European mind, and this
was continually being held up as a model. As it was common
parlance to speak of the "tolerant" Asiatic, so, in the
Chinese, people saw simply the virtuous human being. In
China they thought they had discovered a wholly new moral
world. What this discovery meant for them is clearly stated
by Voltaire. "They have," he says of the Chinese, "per-
fected Moral science, and that is the first of the sciences,"
and he himself described his *Orphelin de la Chine* as "the
Morals of Confucius in five acts."[46] Elsewhere he says:
"The princes of Europe and the men of commerce have, in
all the discoveries in the East, been in search only of wealth,
the philosophers have discovered there a new moral and
physical world."[47] Of Confucius he says: "I have read
his books with attention, I have made extracts from them;
I found that they spoke only of the purest morality. . . .
He appeals only to virtue, he preaches no miracles, there is
nothing in them of ridiculous allegory."[48] And, in another
place, he relates: "I knew a philosopher in whose room the
portrait of Confucius hung by itself, with the following four
verses inscribed below it:

> "*De la seule raison salutaire interprète,*
> *Sans éblouir le monde, éclairant les esprits*
> *Il ne parla qu'en sage, et jamais en prophète*
> *Cependant on le crut, et même en son pays.*"[49]

That which excited Voltaire's admiration was the fact, as
he believed, that the lofty morality of the ancient Chinese
sages had found an echo in the responsible classes of the
population, and had been realized in the ordering of the
State: "One need not be obsessed with the merits of the
Chinese to recognize at least that the organization of their
empire is in truth the best that the world has ever seen, and
moreover the only one founded on paternal authority."[50]
He believed in the high culture of the ruling class of Mandarins, he honoured their teacher Confucius, he knew that the
common folk of China resembled that of Europe, and he
admired the State, which held all these elements together
in an elaborately balanced system, and had wrought them
to a state of rich culture; in China alone had "Theism," the
true religion of the philosopher, "been raised to the position
of a national cult."[51] If Voltaire has to admit that even in

G

China " the People " is not so highly enlightened, this only expresses his general view in social matters: " It has to be admitted that the commonalty ('*le petit peuple*') is as rascally as it is with us, that they haggle as much as we do . . . that they, like ourselves, suffer from a number of ridiculous prejudices, believe in talismans and astrology, as we did for so long." And he wittily adds that there too, while mortal diseases are healed by their doctors as by ours, the lesser evils are only removed by nature.[52] A Voltaire who could speak in this way could not but criticize severely the proselytizing zeal of the European peoples. The Chinese were already in those days content, like all wise men in the world, to worship one god only, while in Europe people were divided between Thomas and Bonaventura, Calvin and Luther, finally between Jansen and Molina.[53] And this Europe dared to reproach China with atheism? " This inconsistency is quite worthy of us, on the one hand to rise in wrath against Bayle for thinking that a society of atheists might possibly maintain itself, and on the other to assert with equal vehemence that the wisest kingdom on the surface of the earth is founded upon atheism."[54] This passion for proselytizing was, he said, a disease peculiar to our climate; it had never been known in distant Asia. Never had these peoples sent missionaries to Europe; we alone exported our opinions as well as our merchandise to the ends of the earth.[55]

" What should our European princes do when they hear of such examples? Admire and blush, but above all imitate."[56]

Voltaire reproached Bossuet for having omitted all mention of the East in his *Discours sur l'histoire universelle ;* for Voltaire, the philosopher of history, the Far East came first in any such review. " If, as a philosopher," he said, " one wishes to instruct oneself about what has taken place on the globe, one must first of all turn one's eyes towards the East, the cradle of all arts, to which the West owes everything." It was, therefore, as a matter of course that Voltaire began his *Essai sur les mœurs* with a long chapter on China.[57]

We shall hardly understand properly Voltaire's pre-dilection for the East, without, at any rate, a brief considera-tion of his *Orphelin de la Chine*, ' Confucian morals in five

acts,' as he called it. While all the music-plays on Chinese
motives, which we previously noticed, were merely intended
to amuse, Voltaire in his *Orphelin* aimed at exercising a moral
influence. This is clear from one of his letters in which he
says expressly that his play has nothing to do with Metastasio's: people might continue to give Metastasio's play as
often as they chose, it could not injure his *Orphelin;* the
two works had nothing but the title in common; and it must
not be imagined that Metastasio's characters are in any way
to be compared with his.[58] Voltaire believed that he could
learn more of Chinese nature from Prémare's translation of
Chinese drama, on which he modelled his *Orphelin*, than
from all the descriptions of the Chinese Empire: "*L'Orphelin
du Chao* is a first-rate document, which is of more use for
understanding the mind of China than all that has been,
or ever will be, related of that vast realm."[59] Accordingly
he hoped to be able to show the French by means of his
drama more of the great virtue of the Chinese than all the
reports of the Jesuits.

Further, Voltaire's *Orphelin* was an answer to Rousseau's
thesis that science and art are destructive of morals.
Voltaire makes the civilization of the Chinese people triumph
over the warlike barbarism of Jenghiz Khan. One is
tempted to suppose that it was on Rousseau's account that
he revived the history of the Tartar barbarians in the Chinese
tale of the *Orphan of Chao*, in order to make his play a direct
contradiction of the former's contention.[60] It is significant
that he placed at the beginning of the first edition of his
drama the well-known letter to Rousseau: "Sir, I have
received your new book against the human race. . . ."

Rousseau replied: "The people receives the writings of
the wise in order to judge them, not to get instruction from
them . . . and I hear plenty of nincompoops criticizing
the *Orphelin*, just because it is applauded, who are quite
incapable of appreciating its faults, let alone its beauties."
From this answer, one might conclude that Rousseau had
understood the attack made upon him.[61]

Voltaire's *Essai sur les mœurs*, which was provoked by
Montesquieu's *Esprit des lois* and the judgment of the East
contained in that work, called forth quite a mass of contemporary writings attacking the China-worship of the day.

The *Encyclopædia* took its views on the Chinese philosophers directly from Voltaire. Diderot writes of them in the *Dictionnaire encyclopédique :* " These peoples, gifted with a ' *consentiment unanime,*' are superior to all other Asiatics in antiquity, intellect, art, wisdom, policy, and in their taste for philosophy; nay, in the judgment of certain authors, they dispute the palm in these matters with the most enlightened peoples of Europe." Equally enthusiastic language is employed by Helvetius in his work *De l'Esprit.*[62] Poivre in his *Travels of a Philosopher*[63] goes so far as to assert that " China offers an enchanting picture of what the whole world might become, if the laws of that empire were to become the laws of all nations. Go to Peking ! Gaze upon the mightiest of mortals; he is the true and perfect image of Heaven." Many minds were possessed by the notion that the salvation of France depended on its permeation with the ennobling spirit of China.*

In the presence of such effusive admiration, cooler and more reserved judgments could not be wanting. In Frederick the Great, for example, when he exchanged ideas about China with Voltaire in his letters, one always detects a slightly ironical attitude towards the enthusiasm of his philosopher friend.

Voltaire had sent to Frederick in 1770 a poetical satire on the *Éloge de Moukden,* written by the Chinese Emperor Chien-lung. He began his satire with the flattering lines: "*Frédéric a plus d'art et connait mieux son monde.*" Frederick thanked him, and observed that he knew Chienlung's poem, which was quite strange to European taste, but might very likely find admirers in Peking.[64] He also told Voltaire that one of the ships of his Emden company, lately returned from China, had brought him a letter in verse from the Chinese Emperor, which had been with difficulty translated. He enclosed a copy of the translation for his Chinese library. He might gather from it how the Russian successes were regarded in China.[65] He accompanied this with a *jeu d'esprit* of his own in the form of a letter in verse purporting to be written by the Emperor of China himself.[66] In 1771 a similar letter followed.[67]

* Grimm in his *Correspondance littéraire*, November, 1785, severely criticizes this desire to " *inoculer l'esprit chinois.*"

In a letter of January 10, 1776, he discusses more seriously Voltaire's views on China: he had been talking over Voltaire's letter with his reader Pauw, but Pauw, it appeared, was more inclined to believe what the former Jesuit, Parennin, who had lived many years in the country, said about China, than the patriarch of Ferney, who had never been there. He, Frederick, left the controversy over the Chinese to the zealous champions of one side or the other; the Emperor of China did not doubt that Europe would some day make up its mind about his nation, and that persons who had never set foot in Peking would at last desist from praising his empire. But the King of Prussia readily admitted his extraordinary ignorance of the manners and customs of the Oriental nations, for he had always confined his attention to Europe, whose affairs occupied him daily. All he knew of the Chinese Emperor were some bad verses, and, unless that monarch had better poets in Peking, no one would be at the pains of learning his language in order to be able to read such verses. Until destiny caused a genius like Voltaire to arise in China, he should not trouble himself further about the matter.[68]

On March 19, 1776, the king writes again: " I leave the Chinese to you and to the Abbé Pauw along with the Indians and the Tartars. The European nations keep my mind sufficiently occupied, so that it has no inclination to desert this most attractive portion of the earth's surface."[69]

Frederick's letter of the 8th of April, 1776, again refers to conversations he had had with Pauw about China. One passage in it has special interest for us, because it shows how clearly the king had perceived the purpose in Voltaire's enthusiasm for China: " I said to him (Pauw): ' But don't you see that the patriarch of Ferney is following the example of Tacitus ?' In order to encourage virtue in his country-men, the Roman historian held up to them as a model the honesty and self-restraint of our Germanic forefathers, who certainly do not deserve to be imitated. In the same way M. de Voltaire is never weary of repeating to his friends across the frontier: ' Only learn from the Chinese the habit of virtuous action, promote agriculture, as they do, and you will see your *landes* of Bordeaux and your Champagne fertilized by the labour of your hands, and bearing rich harvests. Seeing that only one law prevails throughout the whole vast empire of China, must you not desire, oh my countrymen, to imitate them in your little kingdom ?' "70

While Frederick the Great displayed reserve and indifference in regard to the Chinese world, Rousseau viewed it with absolute dislike. He selected the example of China to support his contention that science and art tend to the corruption of manners: " Why go to past times to look for illustrations of a truth, for which we have living witnesses before our eyes ? There is in Asia a vast country in which the sciences are a passport to the highest positions in the State. If the sciences really purified morals, if they really taught men to shed their blood for the fatherland, if they inspired courage, then the people of China would assuredly be wise, free, and invincible. But as a matter of fact, there is no sin to which they are not prone, no crime which is not common amongst them. If neither the ability of its Ministers nor the alleged wisdom of its laws, nor even the numberless multitude of its inhabitants, has been able to protect this realm against subjection by ignorant and rude barbarians, of what service have been all its wise men ?"71

Montesquieu sought, like Rousseau, to make China square with his own dogmas. Setting out from these grounds, he was no more able than Rousseau to penetrate to the true spirit of the East. Voltaire on the contrary was an historian; his outlook was wide, not hemmed in by the limitations of an arbitrary system. He did not approach facts with a demand, but soaked his mind with them.

Montesquieu in his *Esprit des lois* approached China solely from the point of view of his own theory of the State. And the enlightened absolutism which prevailed there conflicted with his political ideal—the triple partition of the powers of government. That was sufficient to determine the attitude towards China of a mind wedded to its own system. In forming his judgment, he took his stand only on the reports of the traders, who were, for the most part, totally unacquainted with Chinese culture, because they came into contact only with Chinese traders, of whom they had nothing better to report than that they were dishonest; and he bluntly asserted that the favourable opinions of the

Jesuits were discredited by the reports of the traders.*[72] He sums up his conclusions as follows: " Our missionaries speak of the vast empire of the Chinese as of a wonderful state, the personification of fear, honour, and virtue; I wonder what sort of virtue there can be in peoples who can only be ruled with the stick !'' Voltaire controverted this ' government by the stick' idea of China in his *Essai sur les mœurs :* " If Montesquieu wishes to convince us that the kingdoms founded in Europe by the Goths, the Gepidæ and the Alans were based upon honour, why will he not allow honour to the Chinese ?" Meanwhile Montesquieu found in his system a further support for his contention; he imputed to the climate of the Far East the state of slavish obedience in which the people lived.[73] It was his opinion that the geographical conditions of China had predetermined its political constitution, of which the foremost principle was " public tranquillity "; and on that principle all later laws had been moulded.[74] Montesquieu's method of enquiry may be illustrated by the following example: he wishes to explain how it was that, in spite of the unfavourable climate, the first Emperors came to make good laws—for the fact he cannot dispute. According to his theory, countries possessing industries require moderate government.[75] There were in his time in China two provinces, Fu-kien and Kwang-si, coming under this category—*i.e.*, of a markedly industrial character. " In them, therefore, as in Holland, the administration was necessarily of a moderate character." In this way the first Chinese Emperors had been obliged, " in spite of the climate, which naturally disposes the inhabitants to slavish obedience,' in spite of the terrors, which always go along with a too extensive empire," to give good laws to the whole of their domains.[76]

In another passage he laments a characteristic which filled all his contemporaries with admiration—the exclusiveness of Chinese culture and the fact that the Chinese lawgivers had succeeded in producing a uniformity in religion, laws, customs, and even in the outward behaviour of the

* It may here be noted that Rousseau also had obviously read nothing about China except the account given by Anson, the Englishman, of an unsuccessful English embassy to the court of Peking.

people—because this circumstance made it difficult for Christianity to take root in the country.[77]

The opposition of the celebrated French man of letters, Grimm, had almost as slender a foundation in fact as that of Rousseau or of Montesquieu. In 1776 he gives so graphic and concise a description of the Chinese legend that his language is worth quoting here: " The Chinese Empire has become in our time the object of special attention and of special study. The missionaries first fascinated public opinion by rose-coloured reports from that distant land, too distant to be able to contradict their falsehoods. Then the philosophers took it up, and drew from it whatever could be of use to them in denouncing and removing the evils they observed in their own country. Thus this country became in a short time the home of wisdom, virtue, and good faith, its government the best possible and the longest established, its morality the loftiest and most beautiful in the known world; its laws, its policy, its art, its industry were likewise such as to serve for a model to all nations of the earth."[78] Grimm clearly saw in China-worship something excessive and in bad taste. He also accepted the judgment of the English Captain Anson. Of him he says: " The famous Captain Anson has, I think, been the first to correct our notions of this Mandarin government of which we have had such flattering pictures painted."*[79] And he comes to the further conclusion that in China the " most terrible despotism " prevails,[80] that the moral doctrines of the Chinese are precisely suitable for a " herd of frightened slaves."[81]

Long before Montesquieu's time Fénelon had pronounced, though from a quite different standpoint, an even more severe judgment on China. After the ruin of his political plans the ageing Fénelon despaired of healing the wounds of Europe. Accordingly he immersed himself in Greek antiquity, in the hope of gaining strength from such studies. Hellas in its prime became his model. Even as a youth he had loved to dwell in thought in the land of Socrates; in later life it became to him a second home.[82]

But at the beginning of the eighteenth century, the

* For Voltaire's adverse judgment of this injured admiral see *Essai sur les mœurs*, chap. i.

growing enthusiasm for the Far East was already beginning
to throw ancient Greece into the shade. For that reason
Fénelon felt constrained to take up an anti-Chinese position.
Thus the longest of the *Dialogues des Morts* took the form of a
discussion between Socrates and Confucius, and bears the
significant sub-title—*Sur la prééminence tant vantée des
Chinois.*[83] Quite at the beginning Socrates draws the
distinction between himself and Confucius. He thinks it
quite unjustifiable to call Confucius the Socrates of China.
For he, Socrates, had never thought of instructing the whole
people in philosophy, because he had never been able to
believe it possible. For that reason he had never sought to
give his thoughts to the public in writing; his one hope
had been by means of the living word to win a few adherents
to whom he might hand on his doctrine. Fénelon makes
his Socrates take up a decidedly sceptical attitude, in order,
by a strong antithesis, to get the better of the acknowledged
optimism of Confucius. "I have deliberately abstained
from writing," says Socrates; "I have even talked too much."
Confucius is from the start driven to the defensive. Socrates
believes that only fear and hope can incite the people to
good actions. Confucius' hope to make the people virtuous
was an idle one. He questions whether the majority of the
people in China has ever been virtuous. Chinese history
has been written in too uncritical a manner to serve as
support for the usual assertions of the contrary view. So
long as the West was not in possession of very exact knowledge of Chinese literature, Chinese history must be for it
a great and beautiful spectacle, but assuredly of very
ambiguous import. In order to save the reputation of
China, Confucius brings forward as witnesses his own
celebrated achievements. But here also Socrates is ready
with his refutation. The invention of printing was surely no
service to be proud of; still less that of gunpowder, which only
served to destroy mankind; Chinese mathematics were lacking
in method; and as for porcelain—"that must be set to the
credit of your soil rather than of your people." Their architecture had no proportion, their painting no composition;
that they had invented lacquer, they owed to their natural
surroundings. Confucius, humbled, asks whether their
great antiquity is not a ground for praise. But Socrates is of

opinion that the original home of the Chinese is not the Far East, but rather one of the regions of Western Asiatic culture, and that, in order to obscure their true origin, Chinese historians had mingled together truth and fable.

In the short concluding sentences of the dialogue the fundamental difference between the Greek and the Chinaman is put in a nutshell. Confucius says that he must first take counsel with one of the oldest emperors, Yao; Socrates replies that for knowledge of early Greece he would not rely upon Cecrops nor even on the Homeric heroes (but only on himself).

The scepticism which Fénelon here displays through the person of Socrates was altogether at variance with the boundless faith of his age in the goodness of human nature, and the universal admiration of China, as the model of a happy and contented people. But it proves that not only in the art of the Rococo, but also in the intellectual productions of the time, an undercurrent deriving from the antique continued to flow.

THE PHYSIOCRATS

THE PHYSIOCRATS

In treating separately the doctrine of the Physiocrats, we do not lose sight of the fact that it is only a political-economical expression of the thought-form and thought-content designated by the general term 'Enlightenment.' The physiocratic doctrine was propagated in the form of a system, the form in which it originated in the brain of its creator, Quesnay; it found disciples who united to form a school, without extending essentially or even giving greater profundity to the ideas of their master; and it disappeared from public discussion, when the French Revolution laid its ban upon the mind of Europe. Quesnay's theory is the 'enlightened' justification of political absolutism. That feature of it which forms a new departure in European thought, and is, therefore, presumably original, is the character of the justification, the fact that it is based on economic considerations. Quesnay's theory became the starting-point of the science generally known to-day as National or Political Economy.

Even before Quesnay's time all sorts of imaginary Utopias, sketches of perfect economic conditions and social conditions generally, had been devised, but they all lacked what Quesnay and his disciples vaunted as the special merit of his system, exact scientific method, *more geometrico*. The revived study of Natural Law harked back to Greco-Roman philosophy.[1] Soon, in order to confirm these theories, men began to have recourse to the widely circulated reports of the Jesuits, which told of such perfect forms of society actually existing in the present. The Jesuit State in Paraguay, and above all the "celestial" order of the Chinese Empire, were continually being held up as models. The pundits of Natural Law of that period fall into two groups. One group, of which Morelly may be taken as typical,[2] went back to Common Possession, as it was assumed to have existed previously to the Social Contract; the other based itself on the Social

101

Contract itself, which sanctified Private Ownership. It was to the latter school that Quesnay belonged.

It must be understood, of course, that Quesnay's life-work cannot possibly be referred to any single circumscribed source. For no idea of historical importance can a clear and unique line of descent be established. Suggestions and influences always cross one another and mix. Quesnay was no exception, but was influenced by numerous contemporary lines of thought.

He was, of course, familiar with Descartes and Locke; they contributed, so to speak, the systematic framework of his doctrine. He saw also the disastrous effects of ' Colbertism ' on his own country, and so recognized that only a decided return to primary production could save France. As a doctor by profession, he had before his eyes in the human body an example of a ' natural organism,' and thus acquired a habit of thought, which he afterwards applied to his political and economic studies.

But all these elements only fell together in a single picture when the example of a state which seemed to embody in perfection these and many other elements—the example of China—was presented to his view. Quesnay was a physician by nature as well as by profession; by which is meant that he found living examples more convincing than historical memories. China had a special attraction for his realistic mind, because it was a living witness of the thing he was seeking and an assurance that the idea of a ' natural order ' was capable of realization, nay, could even point to ways by which it might be realized.

Having seen how completely Quesnay's period came within the radius of Eastern Asiatic influence, it will not surprise us to find that in him too its working was at first rather secret than open. Living in Paris as physician in ordinary to the Pompadour, he had China brought before his notice in a number of ways. To begin with, the Pompadour herself was an enthusiast for that wonderful land, and in her *salons* its strange and attractive culture was a subject keenly discussed. In Paris Jesuit missionaries were always going and coming; and at this very time, about the year 1750, they brought back with them to Paris a Chinese *savant*, Ko, who for thirteen years was a prominent figure in the scientific world, and from whom Quesnay must have learnt many particulars. At the Sorbonne Chinese chronology was discussed. And if Quesnay makes little mention of all this in his writings, that does not prove that it was unknown to him. It would rather seem as if he had deliberately kept silence, in order to appear independent and original.[3] Even in his earliest writings, he expresses such detailed views on China that we have to assume that he was closely acquainted with the literature of the East; and yet, in these same writings, he makes no mention of such sources. It was only in his latest work that he lifted the veil; and if one compares this last work with his first—it was only in his later years that he began to write on economics and political theory—one is surprised by the correspondence of leading conceptions and of the whole structure. Quesnay had already thought out his whole system with all its details—and these in particular were borrowed from China—before the publication of his first treatise.

Above all, his works were written with an immediately practical object. Even the strange labyrinthine lines of the *Tableau économique*, which at first sight might be mistaken for a mystic symbol, were conceived as a representation of living realities, and can only be understood as such. Quesnay's thought has a twofold character. On the one hand it reflects the objective, mathematical mentality of his age; on the other it endeavours to see the totality of things in all their actuality. His attempts to fuse divine order with human order, natural order, as the right way or, in the Chinese phrase, the *Tao* of the world, with actual order— an aim of which the Chinese world perhaps offered the grandest realization—were inspired both by the desire to find a comprehensive mathematical formula for the world and, at the same time, to gain a comprehensive view of cosmic realities. Herein his mentality was akin to that of the Chinese; and from this intellectual kinship sprang his deep love for the Chinese conception of the State and its citizens.

He looked upon the State as a means by which, with the help of the natural economic order—with the help, one might say, of the ' net product '—to bring men back to the original, divine state of nature. His disciple, the elder Mirabeau, in his funeral oration on Quesnay, brings his master into direct relation with the old Chinese political philosopher: " The whole teaching of Confucius," he says, " aimed at restoring to human nature that first radiance, that first beauty, which it had received from Heaven, and which had become obscured by ignorance and passion. He, therefore, exhorted his countrymen to obey the Lord of Heaven, to honour and fear him, to love their neighbours as themselves, to overcome their inclinations, never to make passion the measure of action, but rather to subject it to reason, and not to do, or think, or say, anything contrary to reason. It would be impossible to add anything to this splendid diadem of religious morality; but the most essential part still remained to be done—to bind it upon the brows of earth; and this was the work of our master, whose keen ear caught from the lips of our common mother Nature the secret of the ' net product.' "[4]   Quesnay was, then, spoken of by his own pupils as the direct continuator of the work of Confucius. And we see also why the physiocratic school gave their teacher the honourable title of ' the Confucius of Europe.'

If we take the trouble to separate, in the work of Quesnay, that which is really personal to him, we find that it is principally the method employed in building up all the material of his knowledge into a mathematically clear system. As one of his pupils said: " Method was the speciality of his genius, love of order the ruling passion of his heart."   It is not without significance that the first subject treated by Quesnay in the *Encyclopédie* was that of ' Evidence.'

Everything except his method Quesnay owes to the models he had before him; to Chinese tradition in particular he is indebted for certain basic ideas.

Of this his political testament, 1767, is the most decisive proof. He gave it with intention the title of *Le despotisme de la Chine*. But the work, compared with his first writings, contains no new thought, not an idea with which we are not already familiar. In view of the absolute internal consistency of *all* Quesnay's writings it is unthinkable that he should only have made himself acquainted with Chinese conditions immediately before he planned his last work, in order to reinforce each point in his whole argument with a Chinese example. We have already made mention of various facts which allow it to be inferred with some certainty that he became acquainted with translations of Chinese literature at a much earlier date. Even though he carefully avoided betraying these sources, we have indirect proofs of the fact that he made use of them, that it was not, as was given out,[5] the ancient Greek, but the ancient Chinese, philosophy which stood godmother to his work. In the first place it is important to establish the fact that he rated Chinese philosophy high above the Greek. In speaking of the twenty articles of the *Lun-yü*, he says: " They all deal with good government, virtue and good works; this collection is full of principles and moral sentences, which surpass those of the Seven Sages of Greece."[6] It looks as if Quesnay's rare citations of Greek and Roman philosophy were only made for the sake of drawing upon the recognized sources, the more so as his opponents were fond of appealing for support to the ancient republics. It is possible also that this attitude assumed by Quesnay was largely due to his dislike for purely historical studies, of which he remarked that they only served to satisfy curiosity. Actual things, which were still within reach, he regarded as the most effective confirmations. To this same dislike for Greek antiquity, felt by Quesnay's circle, Baudeau gives expression in the following passage: " Justice and Good Will, for instance, were always lacking in the Greek republics, to which the laws of Natural Order were unknown, and whose annals record an unbroken series of assaults upon the peace and happiness of mankind. Among these everlastingly restless and violent peoples, who were perpetually engaged in bloodshed, who transformed the most fertile regions of the earth into deserts, and covered them with ruins, prevailed the three errors, which I have called the curse of the ' mixed ' states. In view of the miseries which fell to the lot of mankind in this country, no right thinker will continue to acknowledge the formative principles of the ' mixed ' states, principles which are generally regarded as the masterpieces of the Greek philosophers and politicians, and which the moderns have borrowed from them, partly in order to disseminate their doctrines in books, partly to put them to the test in the republics of these latter centuries."[7] How this judgment is to be justified, we will not here enquire. The essential point is that Quesnay shared the opinion held

H

by the philosophical Enlightenment generally: that the end
of the State is the " peace and happiness " of its inhabitants.
And that which excited the admiration of Voltaire and all his
contemporaries, including Quesnay, who took " *despotisme
éclairé* " for their political ideal, was the fact that in China
this form of government had maintained for centuries the
" peace and happiness " of the inhabitants.[8]

But, over and above such a general valuation, Quesnay
must have been, before this, indebted for some of his specific
ideas to Chinese sources. One of his own contemporaries
actually threw it in his teeth that he had no new ideas whatever: " and do not let it be said that these are novelties.
First, such an expression is not suitable; secondly, it con-
tradicts your pretensions to possess a mind, which belongs
to all centuries and all nations; thirdly, the doctrine you
propound, namely, that agriculture is the sole source of
wealth, was held already by Socrates, by Fu-hsi, by Yao, by
Sung and by Confucius."[9]   (Figure 16 and Figure 17.)

While we are on the subject of agriculture, it may be added
that, in 1756, Louis XV, at the suggestion of Quesnay made
through La Pompadour, followed the example of the Chinese
emperors and solemnly guided the plough at the opening of
the Spring tilling; this, it is true, is the only public manifesta-
tion he gave of physiocratic opinions. But it, at least,
proves that the physiocrat doctrine in conjunction with
Chinese tradition was talked of at the French court at that
date, eleven years before *Le despotisme de la Chine* was
written. And, even some years before this, the third volume
of the *Encyclopédie* of Diderot appeared, on which Quesnay
collaborated and which he certainly followed with interest.
It may be assumed that he knew also those sayings of Confucius which are contained in this volume. The sixth saying
runs: " What has Man in common with Heaven? His
intelligent nature. Conformity with this nature gives the
rule of action." And Quesnay wrote in 1765 in very similar
language that " the Natural Order " is " the supreme rule of
all human lawgiving, of all political, economic, and social
action."[10]

In connexion with these sayings the *Encyclopædia* recom-
mends as a source of more detailed information the already
mentioned work of the philosopher Bülffinger.[11] It is

permissible to assume that Quesnay lost no time in making acquaintance with the book. It contained among other things the *Lun-yü* of Confucius, which certainly became of special importance to Quesnay. It may be mentioned in passing that the compilation of the Pétis de la Croix, which contained the laws of Jenghiz Khan, was probably also known to him. If the sources of Quesnay's first works are difficult to trace, the dependence of *Le Despotisme de la Chine* on the political and economic theories of the ancient Chinese is astonishingly clear. One idea in particular—one which is proper to the whole Enlightenment movement—comes up perpetually in this work, the idea that virtue can be taught and learned. Study of the natural laws, the observance of which was supposed to lead to virtue, was, according to the old Confucian view, the highest duty of the statesman, and Quesnay believed that, in China, this duty was complemented by a second, that, namely, of instructing the people in these natural laws. Confucius had said: "I have often gone without food all day and without sleep all night. No matter; to learn is better."[12] And Quesnay wrote: "Only knowledge of the laws can assure the lasting quiet and prosperity of a kingdom,"[13] or, in another place, even more precisely: "The reason must with the help of the intelligence acquire the necessary knowledge."* On the basis of these ideas Quesnay develops his, or rather the Chinese, theory of education. Already in 1765, in his essay, *Du Droit Naturel*, he had formulated the first law of all positive order as follows: "The first positive law, to which all others must conform, is the establishment of public and domestic instruction in the laws of the Natural Order. . . . Without this fundamental institution, government and personal action remain in confusion and disorder; for without the knowledge of the natural laws, which serve as the basis of all human legislation

* Hasbach in his book, *Die allgemeinen philosophischen Grundlagen der von F. de Quesnay und Adam Smith begründeten politischen Oekonomie* (Leipzig, 1890), wrongly attempts to trace a connexion between Quesnay and Cumberland. He was himself obviously not sure of his position. Moreover this attempted interpretation breaks down entirely. For Cumberland speaks only of selfish impulses, which man acquires from the empirical perception that certain actions have favourable, and certain others unfavourable, consequences. He never speaks of what is the kernel of Quesnay's doctrine, that man can, by learning, acquire a knowledge of the natural laws, and is only by virtue of such knowledge capable of good actions.

and as the supreme rule of human conduct, no clear distinction between right and wrong is possible." And in his testament he makes the painful admission that "with the exception of China, the necessity of this institution, which is the foundation of government, has been ignored by all kingdoms." *

Again and again the importance of this education in the natural laws is insisted upon, China cited as a model, and its schools praised. According to Quesnay's account, the Mandarins assemble the inhabitants of even the smallest villages twice a month for 'instruction.' This is based on an 'Instruction Ordinance' which applies to the whole Empire, and which Quesnay regards as important enough to be given in full; he remarks in regard to it: "It will be seen that in these small schools it is not, as generally with us, a mere matter of reading and writing, but that teaching is given at the same time which leads to knowledge. Thus in China the books which contain the fundamental laws of the State are in everybody's hands."[14]

It was this excellent education which, in Quesnay's opinion, enabled China to make itself a model state, completely in harmony with the natural laws: " China is a state founded on science and natural law, whose concrete development it represents."[15] In the introduction to the last chapter of the *Despotisme de la Chine* he says of that despotism: " It is only the method of the Chinese doctrine which should serve as a model to all states."[16] And again Quesnay deplores the fact that here also the Western nations had strayed entirely from the path of natural law.

Even for the more important details of state administration, appeal is made to the example of China. Quesnay's theory of taxation, which plays an important part in his system, had been worked out on the lines of old Chinese laws—probably after the collection of the Pétis de la Croix. He describes as follows the Chinese tax-regulations: " The sum which has to be paid in taxation by the subjects of the Empire is in proportion to the extent of their landed property, account being taken of the quality of the land; for

* It was in pursuit of these ideas of the master that later on Turgot, when he was in office, and Condorcet, following Turgot's example, during the French Revolution promulgated their school programmes.

some time past, it is only the owners of land who pay tax, and not those who merely till the soil."[17] These principles coincide so exactly with his own that, considering the circumstances noted above, we have to assume that the latter were taken from the former. In another passage he analyzes the principles underlying a just system of taxation, and then remarks explicitly: " These are the principles which have now for some centuries so happily guided the government of the Chinese. They draw from them consequences which could with difficulty be put into practice in Europe."[18]

This enthusiastic profession of faith of Quesnay's in the Chinese State had a definite political object. He wished to set the crumbling French monarchy on a new and sound, *i.e.* on a natural, basis, and hoped that such a profession would gain him a better hearing in an age which idealized China. This was perhaps his real reason for at last deciding to reveal the true sources of his inspiration.

His *Tableau économique*, which Voltaire made such excellent fun of in *L'homme aux quarante écus*, was the ingenious translation into mathematics of a Chinese doctrine. Quesnay's own pupil, Baudeau, expressed this connexion clearly in the words: " It actually required several volumes to develop the basic truths, which the *Tableau économique* contains in four lines, just as those four lines were required to explain the sixty-four figures of the Fo-hi."[19] And the same Abbé Baudeau, who was, moreover, the editor of *Ephémerides*, the journal of the physiocratic circle of that time, says in the introduction to his *Philosophie Économique :* " The Chinese are the only known people, whose' philosophers were, from the earliest ages, penetrated by that supreme truth, which they call simply Order, or the Voice of Heaven. They base all measures on this one law: Be guided by the Will of Heaven."[20] What does this signify if not this: that it is only from the ancient Chinese philosophers that the basic principles of all social life can be learned ?

THE AGE OF FEELING

F<small>IG</small>. 22.

THE AGE OF FEELING

T<small>HE</small> character of the transition from ' Enlightenment ' to
its reaction in ' Feeling ' may, in relation to our subject, be
described in some such terms as these. The transition
signified at bottom a rejection of the Cartesian spirit. It
had its beginnings in the Rococo, and it ended in a general
weariness of ' Culture ' and an emotional yearning after
Nature, of which Rousseau is generally regarded as the out-
standing representative. Here it will be sufficient to note
one or two landmarks.

It was the endeavour especially of the generation formed
on Voltaire or Maupertuis to replace the metaphysical method
of Descartes by observation of close-at-hand, human phenomena. Voltaire had compared the metaphysical ideas of
the last generation with stars too far removed from us for
their light any longer to reach us. The human mind returned
from the star-flights of the preceding century to the secrets
of man's own heart. ' *Physique expérimentale de lâme* '
became a current phrase of the time. Rousseau was the
acknowledged spokesman of this relaxed mood, which preceded the French Revolution—a remarkable state of mind
which, after all the wide ranging of the preceding centuries
of discovery, was quite content with the simple and intimate
pleasures afforded by the cultivation of soul. Men were no

longer at pains to "bring distant worlds before them in pompous procession,"[1] but sought for the meaning of life within the narrow circle of the home: "Given a man who lives for the sake of really living, who is happy in himself and pursues the true and simple pleasures, what is such a man doing as he takes his way through the fields in the vicinity of his home? . . . He is not excited by any distant prospect, for enjoyment of the distant springs from the tendency of most men not to be content in themselves; they are for ever longing for what is far away from them. . . . But the man of whom I speak has not this restless habit, and if things are well with him where he is, he does not yearn after other places."[2]

This change of soul in the course of two generations had been preceded—and the connexion is not difficult to seize— by a shifting of the intellectual leadership from France to England. By 1750, the word 'Anglomania' already denoted a European fact. The relation of Rousseau to Richardson's 'Clarissa' is good evidence of this.

The true image, the outward symbol, which this sentimentalism created for itself was the new style in gardens. By virtue of its spiritual development England was destined to supersede the old Louis XIV style of garden. The genial theism of Shaftesbury had brought him to a glorification of unspoiled Nature. "Even the rude rocks, the mossy caverns, the irregular unwrought grottos and broken falls of water with all the horrid graces of the wilderness itself, as representing Nature more, will be the more engaging, and appear with a magnificence beyond the formal mockery of princely gardens."[3] And even in 1712, Addison, with a reference to Shaftesbury's words, called the Chinese to witness that in natural out-of-doors surroundings, Nature alone, and not Art, can be left to indulge its own genius. So we come back to the more immediate subject of our enquiry. "The Chinese," says Addison, "ridicule our plantations, which are laid out by the rule and line; because they say anyone may place trees in equal rows and uniform figures. They choose rather to show a genius in works of this nature, and, therefore, always conceal the art by which they direct themselves."[4] About the same time Pope in the *Guardian* confessed to similar ideas, and set an example by destroying his beautiful, geometrically laid out garden at Twickenham to make place for the new style. And Addison went so far in his revolt against the prim order of the old style as to plant his new garden promiscuously with vegetables, flowers, fruit-trees, and forest-trees.

Once started by Pope and Addison, the new development advanced rapidly in England. Old gardens disappeared, and new ones, at first scantily enough clothed, took their place. People prided themselves on being in the fashion. The art-critic, Home, wrote at the time: " The fine arts are still far from perfection with us. However, they are progressing, though, if we except that of the garden, but slowly." Gardening was indeed quite regarded as one of the arts. Thomas Whately places it above painting, because " Reality is superior to a representation."[5]

Opinions may differ as to whether the English arrived at these ideas independently or took their cue from China. Thomas Gray, a contemporary witness, decides for the former alternative. " The only proof," he writes, " of our original talent in matter of pleasure " is " our skill in gardening, or rather laying out grounds: and this is no small honour to us, since neither Italy nor France have ever had the least notion of it, nor yet do at all comprehend it when they see it. . . . Assuredly . . . we had only nature for a model . . . the art was born among us; and it is sure that there was nothing in Europe like it; and as sure we then had no information on this head from China at all."[6]   In this last statement Gray is certainly wrong. Addison's evidence has already been given. And before him the widely read Le Comte had already, in 1696, written about Chinese gardens.[7] A little later Kämpfer also, in his no less well-known *History of Japan*, described this Oriental art.[8]   He was followed in 1735 by Du Halde,[9] and a wide circulation was obtained by Père Attiret's letter of 1747, which delighted all garden-lovers with its enthusiastic description of the Chinese Summer Palace Yüan-ming-yüan.[10]   (Figure 18 and Figure 19.)   This letter in particular gave a further stimulus to the whole movement in England. It was discussed at length in the *Lettres d'une Société* of 1751,[11] was reproduced in outline by Voltaire,[12] and incorporated by Latapie in his translation of Whately's work on English gardens.[13]   All the treatises which appeared in connexion with the fashion for Chinese gardens had reference to it.

In the movement which now developed, two tendencies can be distinguished—a more extreme, which banished art from the garden altogether, and a middle line, which would suffer neither unadulterated nature, nor art, to reign supreme. No evidence is needed to show that at first it was the former tendency, the strong reaction against the exaggerated constraints of the Louis XIV type of garden, which held the field. There was a revolution in style which Schiller described in the following terms: "From the severe discipline of the architect, it (the art of gardening) fled to the liberty of the poet, suddenly exchanged the hardest slavery for the wildest licence, and would accept laws from the imagination alone."[14] People began at once to lay out natural gardens, quite undistinguished from their surroundings. Even garden-walls were avoided, so that the eye might range unimpeded over the landscape beyond. Two things, however, were lacking to these gardens, and those, precisely the things which the 'man of feeling' was in search of—first, that distinction from the surrounding country, without which they might be natural, but could not be gardens; secondly, variety. What the men of those days needed, in order to provide a variety of delights for their varying moods, was a garden which should embody in itself both nature and art. The function of art should have been to combine unobtrusively in a manifold but unified plan the most various natural forms, as vehicles of so many different emotional suggestions. The art-theory of the garden had to develop into a kind of Metaphysic, by the aid of which the artist might make of the garden an inexhaustible source of varied sentimental reactions.[15]

Such an art found its models in the Chinese gardens. Chambers, architect to the King of England, first made them known in Europe. As a young man, he had travelled to China in the service of the East India Company of Sweden. Later in life, he paid a second visit to the Far East, as architect of the King of England, and, from this journey, he brought back the ideas which he put on paper in his *Essay on Oriental Gardening*.[16] This essay contained, besides its commendation of the Chinese garden, his reasons for rejecting

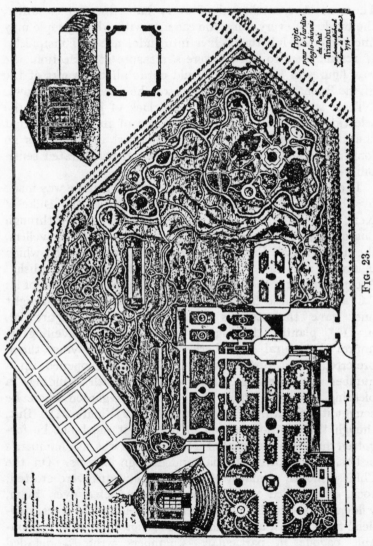

Projet
pour le Jardin
Anglo-chinois
du Petit
Trianon.

FIG. 23.

the pure landscape-garden, such as he found it on his return to England. "Both artists and connoisseurs," he wrote, " seem to me to lay too much stress on nature and simplicity. These are the catchword of every half-educated twaddler, the burden of every song, the cadence with which people may unconsciously lull themselves into indolence and insipidity. If resemblance to nature were a measure of perfection, the wax figures in Fleet Street would outdo all the works of the divine Buonarotti." And the reasons he gives are as follows: "There is so little variety and such lack of judgment in the selection of the objects, such poverty of imagination, that the visitor is bored to death." This sort of thing was no longer a robust return to nature, but an exaggerated sensibility—'sentimentality' in fact.

The first example of a Chinese garden in Europe was made by Chambers in Kew Garden, the property of the Duke of Kent (1750–1759). These grounds became, partly through Chambers's essay, partly through the reports of travellers, the model for all European gardens in the new style, which in France soon came to be known as the "Chinese-English." A contemporary, the art-critic Hirschfeld of Kiel, says of it: "Chambers chose here the curved instead of the straight line, gave the streams a winding course (Figure 20, p. 1I7), planted the higher ground without levelling it, improved natural shrubberies without destroying them, preferred green turf to sandy open spaces, opened up a number of charming vistas, ennobled with buildings a pleasing grove—in short, Kent found his garden where he sought it, in nature."[17] (Figure 20 and Figure 21). But, though there is no mention of it here, it must not be forgotten that even the Duke of Kent's garden was, at Chambers's orders, filled with artificial and foreign objects. On the Chinese model, miniature hills and mountains were erected, rocks were piled up, and cascades conducted over them, wildernesses were laid out, there were clumps of trees, artificial rocks, ruins, and buildings of foreign type—the fashionable pagoda in particular. Chambers wrote a detailed description of the Kew Gardens pagoda, which was his own work, and illustrated it with engravings.[18] It is represented there as having nine storeys and rising to a height of one hundred and sixty feet. Each storey has a Chinese roof with projecting eaves.   The corners of the roofs are adorned with eighty dragons, all covered with a glaze of various colours.   The fact is pointed to with pride that in some directions the pagoda commands a view of forty miles. This Kew Gardens pagoda was soon copied in a number of places; the best-known of these copies are those of Het Loo in Holland, and of Chanteloup on the Loire, on a property belonging to the Duc de Choiseul.[19]   In the ' *Englischer Garten* ' at Munich, the Chinese Tower remains to witness to this fashion.

It was in France that Chambers's ideas were first taken up. From 1760 on, all new gardens were laid out on the model of Kew and Stowe.[20]   It was a picture of Stowe which in 1759 led to the translation into French of Thompson's *Seasons*.[21]   In 1762 Mme. du Boccage, on the strength of her experiences of Stowe and Richmond, criticized French taste as " *trop symmétrisé*."[22]   Holbach brought back with him to France from his English tour the praises of the Chinese-English gardens.[23]   Mme. Roland was full of enthusiasm for the new style.   Grosley's descriptions of London included detailed accounts of Kew and Stowe,[24] as did also the *Observations de Londres et de ses Environs* of Lacombe;[25] their praises are to be read in the works of Baron von Wimpfen,[26] of Cambry,[27] Morel, F. de Hartig,[28] in Whately,[29] and in the *Idylls* of Delille.[30]

Meanwhile Chambers was not ashamed to cite historical examples in defence of his exotic tastes: Hadrian, who was himself an architect, had caused various buildings in the Egyptian and other styles to be erected at his country seat at Tivoli.   He, Chambers, regarded such pretty little buildings in gardens as the finery of architecture, and if such decorative objects might be collected in Curio-cabinets, why should they not be made an ingredient in the " composition of an improved *genre* "?   Accordingly around the dominant pagoda[31] at Kew he grouped a 'House of Confucius' on the edge of the lake, as representative of Chinese taste, (Figure 14, facing p. 65), a mosque, a Roman triumphal arch— a tribute to the already reawakened taste for the antique— an Alhambra and a Gothic building with a cathedral-like façade.[32]   Gothic ruins were just then coming into fashion, and it is curious to observe how Chinese and Gothic were

actually combined in one style. In England appeared a
book of examples of Gothic architecture, in which some
of the plates are strongly reminiscent of Chinese garden-
buildings depicted in Halfpenny's *Shelters, Porticoes and
Pavilions* (Figure 23, p. 117). By 'Chinese' and
'Gothic' were understood styles with free, flamboyant
curves in the roofs and balconies; 'Chinese-Gothic' became
an accepted term. Thus in the *Triumph of Sentiment*
Goethe calls the artificial grottos of the English garden
'Chinese-Gothic.'[33]

The protest against this overloading of the garden with
all manner of embellishments was continuous. Thus Weise
wrote:

"The garden is decked out bravely, here statues and there
cascades, the whole company of the gods, here fauns, there
naiads, and beautiful nymphs bathing, and gold sent from
the Ganges, and shell-work and gilded vases, and porcelain
on close-shaven swards, and trellises and—one thing only
I miss: is it possible that anything is lacking? Nothing
except—Nature!"*

Rousseau likewise missed the simplicity of nature in the
museum of the Chinese garden. "I should like men's
recreations always to be of a light and simple character," he
says;[35] but in the Chinese gardens nature was presented in
a thousand different guises, and yet taken as a whole it was
not nature.

But the 'men of feeling' replied: "Rousseau, it seems,
would like to banish the whole idea of Art from gardens.
Why does he not rather reject gardens altogether? His
elysium is a beautiful spot to which a thinker may retire,
who desires not entertainment but refreshment. We make
gardens in order to be able to enjoy the beauties of nature
within a limited space and in detail, not in order to see her

---

* " *Der Garten ist sehr schön geschmückt,*
        Hier Statuen und dort Kaskaden,
        Die ganze Götterzunft, hier Faunen, dort Najaden,
        Und schöne Nymphen, die sich baden,
        Und Gold vom Ganges hergeschickt,
        Und Muschelwerk und güldne Vasen,
        Und Porzellan auf aufgeschnittenem Rasen,
        Und Gitterwerk und—eines such' ich nur :
        Ist's möglich dass was fehlt? Nichts weiter
                                    als—Natur !"[34]

as a whole."[36] The special charm of a garden, in its artistic aspect, consisted for the men of that period in its power to attune the mind to all moods—sublime, grave, gay, passionate —in varied succession. It was in this character that the new style won its way all over Europe.

In Germany it became domiciled twenty years later than in France. The man who practically introduced it there was the landscape-gardener, F. L. Sekell, whom the Elector Max Josef IV sent in 1773 to study under Chambers the new style in garden-craft and architecture.[37] Frederick the Great also, in his latter years, showed a great predilection for the new style.[38] The most ambitious example of the 'Chinese-English' garden in Germany is that of Wilhelmshöhe near Kassel: and of this we will give a few details.

The Landgrave of Kassel had conceived the idea of establishing a colony in the form of a Chinese village. According to Chambers, such a settlement should consist of scattered houses grouped round a temple; and there must be, of course, a stream of water with an arched Chinese bridge. At Weissenstein, on the south side of the Wilhelmshöhe lake, all the natural conditions for a Chinese village were ready to hand. In 1781, the building was begun. The cottages were almost all of them, in Chinese fashion, of one storey. The style of architecture was well imitated, as may be seen from a contemporary piece of faïence.[39] The village was christened 'Moulang,'[40] and the little piece of water at the foot of the hill, on which the village lay, 'Hu-Kiang.' An estate-book gives us details of the extent of the settlement. It consisted of the following buildings: (1) A two-storeyed dwelling-house for the tenant farmer; (2) "a long Chinese 'sallong' with two cabinets for dining- and ball-room"; (3) two cottages adjoining; (4) a large dairy; (5) a shepherd's house; (7 and 8) two cow-houses; (9) a long-shaped cottage with two compartments; (10) a barn; (11) "a large new building," formerly the "Spanish sheep-stable"; (12) five small cottages.

It is clear from this inventory that the settlement also served practical purposes. It was used for dairy-work, which was a favourite hobby of those days. And as they had no Chinese women, they contented themselves with black women as milkmaids. However, the scattered character of

I

the colony made it unsuitable for dairying, so that the next Elector decided to let the cottages.

Most of them have now disappeared, but the so-called ' pagoda,' once the centre-piece of the design, is still to be seen. It is a small, round temple with the typical double roof; in the interior is a coloured figure of a Bonze under a baldaquin, with two priests standing beside him on little tables. In 1783, a bronze altar of incense was added and a ' Bibliothèque postiche ' with the titles of Chinese works.

Further, the place of the present ' Devil's Bridge ' was occupied originally by one of the Chinese wooden bridges so common at the time, and of which Brentano speaks in his novel *Godwin* as " Chinese bridges spanning roaring torrents."

In the course of years the grounds received various additions. In 1778, a plantation of mulberry-trees was made, probably in connexion with the village, though its actual position cannot now be determined. The Elector Jerome had a Chinese gallery built connecting the Northern wing of the palace with the door of the ball-room on the South; to judge from the plan, which has been preserved, this was one of the best imitations of Chinese architecture of the century.[41] Before that time the successor of the Elector who built Moulang had done away with the old regular park of Wilhelmshöhe, and replaced it by a new one in the English style.

It is not uninteresting to observe how, in Germany of course, a philosophy, a special æsthetic, of the new garden style arose.

First, Ludwig A. Unzer wrote *On Chinese Gardens*.[42] He treats them as the model of all garden art. " The English nation, of which one may fairly say that it has more appreciation of the sublimer kind of beauty than others, has long since convinced itself of the superiority of Chinese taste in the planning of gardens."[43] The winding curves of the Chinese gardens he takes to be an expression of mobility of mind: " They carry their love of the serpentine line, which they rightly hold to possess more life and movement than the right line, so far as to apply it not only to their footpaths, their rock-stairways, their valleys, and water-channels, but even to their bridges." (Figure 24 and Figure 25.) The enviable power which the Chinese possessed of arousing in the human soul, through their gardens, an uninterrupted succession of lively feelings is described in the following terms: " The Chinese artists distinguish three kinds of prospects or effects, which they think suitable for gardens: first, pleasing spectacles which stir the mind to thought, among which they include even such as provoke a gentle melancholy; secondly, scenes which inspire a sort of alarm and fear; and thirdly, such as are calculated to produce astonishment, or at once to deceive and enchant the eye."[44] " Echoes tenfold repeated, which they arrange in the cleverest manner, make such a spot quite a source of inspiration."[45] Waterfalls dash one into another, while charred ruins hard by heighten the sense of terror. But to terrible scenes pleasing ones at once succeed, "and these after all must always form the central feature of a garden."[46]

" To soft, dark colours they oppose brilliant and lively ones, simple forms to composite. In the end, by an arrangement in which taste is their only rule, they produce a whole, in which the parts are noticeably distinguished one from another, but which in its total effect delights us with the most refined sense of harmony."[47] Objects of unusual form are preferred, because they increase the garden's capacity to stimulate feeling: " In particular, gnarled and knotted tree-trunks are frequently met with in their gardens, because they have a special power of arresting the attention."[48]

We might multiply passages from this book which betray a relation between the writer's own æsthetic demands and Chinese garden-craft. We will content ourselves with the final summing up. He counsels Europeans to assimilate themselves to " the masculine taste of the Chinese." " We shall not attain to perfection in this matter," he says, " until we make the manner of this nation our own. We need have no shame about doing so." " We have no taste," says Lessing (in the Preface to his *Dramaturgie*), " if we have only a one-sided taste. Let us say further: True taste prizes the beautiful, wherever it finds it. *Externo robore crescit.*"[49]

Ideas similar to these, though expressed in the form of a philosophic system, are to be found in the work of the Kiel Professor of Æsthetic, C. S. E. Hirschfeld. For him, as for the Chinese, the garden was merely an arrangement for producing emotions. Hirschfeld attempts by means of a

rigorous self-examination to make a logical classification of
the emotions of the Garden: " The mountain heights excite
wonder and, by their majestic appearance, attune the soul
to a solemn exaltation, to awe and admiration. The hill,
with its gracefully curved contours, produces gaiety and
cheerfulness; a hollow in the landscape is the dwelling-place
of solitude and peace; it disposes to melancholy, silent con-
templation and *rêverie ;* the crag has power to arouse wonder,
awe, even horror and alarm, and to lend an heroic character
to the landscape. . . . On the other hand, liveliness, gaiety,
merriment are qualities belonging to the lighter under-
growths, to the grove. The meadow suggests only moderate
movement, it calls up images of Arcadian shepherds."[50]
Contrast, as cultivated in the Chinese garden, was for
Hirschfeld also the first principle of this art.

What he says of the way in which the taste for Chinese
gardens spread through Europe is the more valuable in that
we scarcely have any living witnesses left: " Of all the gardens
of all the different parts of the world, none has excited more
attention than the Chinese, or that which has been so charm-
ingly described as such. So much is certain, that the Englishman is possessed by a strong prejudice in favour of this kind
of garden, and that the Frenchman, and with him the German,
is beginning to abandon himself to this prejudice. What
people ask for now is not gardens laid out according to their
own ideas, or in better taste than the old, but Chinese or
Chinese-English gardens."[51] This development was obviously
proceeding at such a rapid pace that Hirschfeld was alarmed
lest, in their hurry to imitate, the European peoples might
forget their own cunning.[52]

Every movement, be it one of world-wide importance or
merely a passing fashion, finds in this way sooner or later its
systematizer or collector, who translates it into folio volumes
and preserves it for posterity. And the movement which
bore the standard of the English-Chinese garden was no
exception to the rule. It had its *Encyclopædia*[53] containing
a large collection of illustrations and expressly intended
" to promote the progress of Garden-craft, since everyone
knows that the English garden is only an imitation of the
Chinese."

However, by the year 1787, when this work was completed,

the movement had already ceased to be predominant, first in England, and afterwards in France and Germany. In Holland, where the formal garden went out of fashion only at the beginning of the following century, the development was delayed for some decades.

Everywhere the healthy, simple feeling for nature reasserted itself. In England, there was a reaction against Chambers. As early as 1767, William Mason had published his first verses on *The English Garden*, which charge Chambers with an excessive multiplication of architectural features and describe his decorative elaborations as " affected." The simple landscape-garden came into its own again after this Chinese interlude, and has maintained its supremacy to this day. Repton was its champion in England, and he displaced Chambers.

In this connexion we must not omit to mention the appearance of an artistic technique, which at that time became popular in Europe, an offspring of the Age of Feeling, like the Chinese garden, and, like it also, obviously borrowed from China. Water-colour painting grew out of the need for a new rendering of landscape corresponding to the new feeling for Nature.[54] Once more, no explanation is required of the fact that the first landscape-painter to employ this medium was an Englishman: John Robert Cozens (d. 1794).

In their colouring the landscapes of this painter surprise us by their affinity with Chinese art. Cozens used brown and grey for the ground-tones with a touch of blue and red for the lights. But he first put in the outlines in Chinese ink. Since he laid on the ink, as he did all his other colours, with the brush and not with the pen, he developed a technique, which even in detail corresponded to the Chinese method of landscape-painting.*[55]

While Cozens, faithful to his Chinese models, confined himself to landscape, his successors went on to paint figures in water-colour. Joshua Christall (d. 1847) and Henry Liversedge (d. 1832) may be here mentioned. In their work

* Chinese ink was also used in the preliminary stages of Miniature-painting, which likewise only attained its charming delicacy during the Rococo. The student was taught 'to go on working with Chinese ink until he had acquired perfect delicacy and sureness of touch with the brush. Only then was he allowed to proceed to colour.

the colouring is noticeably stronger. And Turner, about 1800, gave up the use of Chinese ink.

It is difficult to decide—as it is in many of the matters which concern our enquiry—how far Chinese influence went in directing the development of European technique in painting; we can only be certain that such influence existed.

As an indication of the change in spiritual attitude which came after the Enlightenment, it may be noted that it was at that time that the first translations from the literature of Chinese Nature-mysticism were made. The earliest European translation of Lao Tzŭ appeared about 1750. It is preserved only in the form of a Latin MS. at the India Office in London, and was probably the work of a Jesuit missionary.[56] Afterwards, Rémusat (to whom W. von Humboldt owed his knowledge of Chinese) wrote various treatises on Lao Tzŭ, and, in 1824, translated four chapters of his work.[57] Since that time Lao Tzŭ has come more and more to take rank alongside of Kung Fu-tzŭ, and to-day he holds the field in much the same degree as Kung did two hundred years ago.

We see then that the 'Age of Feeling' presents no less full a picture of relations with China than did the 'Enlightenment' and the 'Rococo.'

GOETHE

GOETHE

In saying something of Goethe in this connexion, we are fully aware that we can add nothing new or important to the picture of that great personality. On the other hand, we believe that even in the lightest utterances of genius something of its essence is to be discovered. If we reconstruct for ourselves Goethe's opinion of China mosaic-wise from remarks scattered over his whole life, we find that even here the ripeness of his development reveals itself, that he had a deeper insight into the nature of the East—although he had no occasion to emphasize it—than the whole century which preceded him, and that he may therefore fitly form the conclusion of this enquiry.

A certain amount of research-work pertinent to our subject lies ready to hand. Biedermann has published among his Goethe-researches some good critical studies of the sources of certain works of Goethe, which betray relations with China.[1] In his 1879 papers, he tries to trace back to a Chinese motive the unfinished tragedy *Elpenor;* in the *New Series* of 1886, he carries the enquiry a step further. The same volume contains a study of sources for the *Chinesisch-deutsche Jahres- und Tageszeiten* (Chinese-German Yearly and Daily Times). Finally in the *Further Series* of 1899 he makes use of Zarncke's critical work[2] to clarify his views on *Elpenor*, and concludes with a more comprehensive account of Goethe's whole connexion with China literature.

In this work we are not directly concerned with the study of sources; our first business is to show what Goethe saw of China and how he saw it; and how his ideas can be explained in the light of his changing outlook on things in general.

Goethe belonged, with more than the half of his life, to the eighteenth century, a century distinguished by the great number of conflicting spiritual forces at work in it. These oppositions may all be reduced to the one great antithesis, to which all lesser tendencies became subservient, of the Classic and the Romantic. Into the conflict between these two principles Goethe was born.

Goethe's attitude towards the romantic *chinoiserie* of his contemporaries—romanticism and love for the exotic are apt to go together—plays no special part in his relation to Romanticism generally. And yet it has sufficient bearing on this general relation to deserve not to be altogether passed over; particularly as for Goethe, in his old age, the name of China was associated with quite another train of thought.

The change in Goethe's judgment of China took place about the time of Schiller's death. Whereas, up to that time, Goethe had been acquainted only with the external aspects of the Chinese, he now became aware of the ' idea ' of Chinese culture, its real essence. The particular case is an illustration of the relative way in which Goethe approached things, taking from them just so much as answered to the particular phase of his intellectual evolution.

Even in his early youth he received external impressions of the Chinese. In *Dichtung und Wahrheit* he tells of the unbounded wrath of his father evoked by his " casting aside certain Chinese hangings " in the paternal mansion.[3] He refers no doubt to the Peking-hangings in the house on the *Hirschgraben*, which are mentioned in another passage.[4] Even as an elderly man, at the time when he was writing down the reminiscences of his youth, Goethe associated with these hangings—and this is the point to be noticed—" certain elaborately carved mirror-frames," which he condemned in the same breath with the Chinese work. Clearly the Chinese and the flamboyant character of the Rococo made a kindred impression on his mind. With this bracketing of the two styles we may compare the equation ' fantastical-Chinese,' which also occurs in *Dichtung und Wahrheit*. He is speaking of wall-hangings, " on which sometimes Chinese and fantastical, sometimes natural flowers were depicted."[5] This opposition of ' Chinese-fantastical ' to ' natural ' deserves notice. It is of a piece with the great antithesis which he set up in so many different forms—though his own preference is always clear enough—and which he expressed so trenchantly in the hearing of Eckenstein, " The Classical I call the healthy and the Romantic the morbid." Goethe had

in his youth abundant opportunity, in the course of social
intercourse, to observe the exotic fancies of the eighteenth
century. In the wealthy houses of the ' Patricians ' of his
native town many richly decorated lacquer cabinets were to
be found, and their over-refined, sentimental style is castigated
by him in the *Triumph of Sentiment*. (Figure 26.)

It is not until his Strassburg time that we again hear of
his coming into contact with things Chinese. In a note in
his Strassburg *Ephemerides* of the year 1770 he sets down
among books to be read a translation of the six Chinese
classics—" containing didactic, ethical and philosophical
matter "; but whether he made any serious study of this is
uncertain. The reference is obviously to the translation
published in 1711 by the Jesuit Father Noël of the *Sex libri
classici sinensis*.

His time in Strassburg before his meeting with Herder
was filled up with all manner of alchemistic studies—
Paracelsus for example ! With a like object the youthful
student plunged into the literature of Mysticism. What he
was at bottom in search of was the marvellous, the never-
yet-discovered something, which should reveal to him the
ultimate unity of things. And so, when he chanced upon
this work, nobody knows how, it took his fancy as emanating
from an, as yet, unexplained and mysterious world. But
the little note leads to nothing. Herder came into Goethe's
life and diverted his intellectual development into another
channel. (In his *Voices of the Peoples* Herder did not include
any Chinese poetry.)

In 1773 we find in Goethe's review of the *Musenalmanach*
for that year, which was published in the *Frankfurter
gelehrten Anzeigen*, a characteristic remark on a ' Chinese
poem ' by Unzer. " Mr. Unzer's work is inlaid work, made
up of Chinese knick-knacks, which would be quite in place
on tea-trays and toilet-boxes."[6] Goethe felt these little
Chinese ' conceits ' as pretty trifles to be enjoyed for a
moment, but devoid of any deeper significance.

In the *Triumph of Sentiment*, in which Goethe took leave
of his own sentimental phase, the Chinese becomes an expression of the Romantic. In certain places Goethe actually
uses it as a symbolical background. The whole of the Second
Act is played in a room " decorated in Chinese taste, the

back-scene yellow with brightly coloured figures." We may
recall also the Prologue to the Fourth Act, which contains
the following satirical description of the Chinese garden:

" *As I was saying : to have the perfect park*
hardly a touch is needed.
We have hollows and heights,
samples of every shrub that grows,
winding paths, waterfalls, pools,
pagodas, caverns, greenswards, rocks and chasms,
quantities of mignonnette and other fragrant things,
gloomy pines, Babylonian willow-trees, ruins,
hermits in holes, shepherds on the green,
mosques and towers with cabinets,
of moss most uncomfortable beds,
obelisks, labyrinths, triumphal arches and arcades,
fishermen's huts, pavilions for bathing,
*Chinese-Gothic grottos, kiosques and ' tings.' "**

Here again the juxtaposition ' Chinese-Gothic ' surprises
us. For Goethe's æsthetic feeling, there was an essential
division between the Classical and everything non-Classical.
This particular combination of ' Chinese-Gothic ' was not,
however, peculiar to Goethe. As we have seen elsewhere,
the men of his time frequently lumped the two styles together; they saw in both a restless play of sinuous, con-
voluted line, which contrasted with the sedate tranquillity
and simplicity of classical forms.

In this connexion we will anticipate two later judgments
of Goethe on the Chinese garden. In the *Paralipomena on
Dilettantism*, in which Schiller and Goethe collaborated, we
read: "English taste has that foundation in the useful, which
the French has to sacrifice. Mimicry of English taste has
the appearance of the useful, Chinese taste."[8] That expresses Goethe's real opinion of the Chinese garden. He

---

* Was ich sagen wollte: zum vollkommenenen Park
Wird uns wenig mehr abgehn.
Wir haben Tiefen und Höhen,
Eine Musterkarte von allem Gesträuche,
Krumme Gänge, Wasserfälle, Teiche,
Pagoden, Höhlen, Wieschen, Felsen und Klüfte,
Eine Menge Reseda und andres Gedüfte,
Weimutsfichten, babylonische Weiden, Ruinen,
Einsiedler in Löchern, Schäfer im Grünen,
Moscheen und Türme mit Kabinetten,
Von Moos sehr unbequeme Betten,
Obelisken, Labyrinthe, Triumphbogen, Arkaden,
Fischerhütten, Pavillons zum Baden,
Chinesisch-gotische Grotten, Kioske, Tings.[7]

regarded it as a mongrel form—something between the old, stiff, Baroque garden and pure landscape-gardening. His ideal was a naturally grown garden, such as he desiderates in the *Wahlverwandschaften :* " No one can feel himself at ease in a garden, unless it resembles the open country; there should be nothing to remind us of art and constraint; we want to breathe an absolutely free air." Biedermann is mistaken therefore in saying that, in the Park at Weimar, Goethe created " a landscape-garden in the grandest Chinese style, in the spirit of Chinese art."[9] Obviously Biedermann is confusing the Chinese with the pure landscape-garden, which in the last decade of the eighteenth century had already almost taken the place of the former.

Not long after the *Triumph of Sentiment* came the remarkable fragment of a tragedy, *Elpenor*, which at first sight might seem to have little to connect it with our subject. A fragment always has a special attractiveness, just because the problem is left unsolved. But few fragments have aroused so much interest as this of *Elpenor*. Schiller was strongly attracted by it. When Goethe sent him the piece to criticize in 1798, he feels inclined to judge it more favourably than the author himself, " for," says he, " it is one of those works which carry one, or urge one, beyond the subject itself straight to the mentality of its author." In 1805, only a short while before his death, he writes to Goethe: " Do not forget to send me *Elpenor*." As we learn from Riemer, Zelter was equally fond of the piece, and the feeling was shared by Riemer himself: " Like Schiller and Zelter I had a special affection for this fragment." But at the same time he has unfortunately to confess: " I neglected at the time, or had not the sense, to enquire how Goethe had come to treat this subject, and what original had inspired him."[10]

Among more recent studies of Goethe three in particular have endeavoured to discover the source of *Elpenor*— Biedermann, in the first two series of his *Goetheforschungen;* Zarncke, in his *Goethe-Schriften*, and Ellinger in *Ueber Goethes Elpenor*, in the sixth volume of the *Goethe-Jahrbuch*.[11] The last two works arose out of a dispute with Biedermann. Biedermann in his first essay had asserted the claims of the Chinese drama, *The Little Orphan of the House of Chao*, to be the source of *Elpenor*. According to this theory, Goethe's

own experience would form only the sentimental undertone
of the drama; we are reminded of what Schiller said—that
there was a " certain femininity of feeling " about the play.
It dates from the time of Goethe's close relations with Frau
von Stein.

Ellinger rather superficially attempted to show that
Hamlet had provided the suggestion; the reasons he gives
are that Goethe wrote the *Elpenor* at the same time as the
discussion on *Hamlet* in *Wilhelm Meister*. Goethe, he thinks,
wished " to show us a character like that of Hamlet, before
destiny had converted him into a sullen, gloomy and mis-
anthropic dreamer." But as Goethe did not see Hamlet
at all in this light, there was no reason why he should wish
to provide him with such a previous history.

More serious is Zarncke's reply. He accepts the Chinese
play as source for *Elpenor*, but regards it as an insufficient
explanation by itself. He thinks he has discovered a further
source in the *Antiope* of the eighth fable of Hyginus. Biedermann agrees with him on this point, but on new grounds.
Goethe, he argues, could not possibly leave the piece in
Chinese cultural surroundings, but was obliged to find a new
world in which to place the action, and so had hit upon the
fables of Hyginus, which he was fond of dipping into. Hence
the Greek form given to the Chinese matter.

Here we have a foundation on which we can attempt to
build up for ourselves a history of the origin of *Elpenor*.
From a note in his diary of January 10, 1781, it appears that
at that time Goethe had been reading Du Halde's *Detailed
Description of the Chinese Empire*, and had there come across
a Chinese play and also a Chinese story, which greatly
delighted him. The play was *The Little Orphan of the House of
Chao*, of which Du Halde had incorporated in his work
Father Prémare's translation. On August 11 of the same
year, the diary records the beginning of *Elpenor*. Again,
on August 19, we know that he was working at the play;
both the diary and a letter to Frau von Stein witness to this.
Then we hear nothing more until March 1, 1783. On that
day, Goethe writes to Frau von Stein that he has a play on
the stocks, and from a letter of March 5, it is clear that this
was *Elpenor*. On March 3, he writes to Knebel: " I had
hoped to get the piece, of which you know the beginning,

written before the departure of the Duchess, but it is impossible. The old plan was unsatisfactory and I had to recast it from the beginning. I go on quietly, and hope it will not come too late." On March 5, he announced to Frau von Stein the completion of the Second Act, and there the work was finally broken off.

So far then, the development was as follows: For the fact that the two Chinese pieces must have made an unusual impression on Goethe we have not only his own testimony but that of Ampère. He wrote on May 23, 1827, to his friend Madame Récamier that Goethe remembered quite well the incidents of the Chinese story (the one given by Du Halde), which he had read half a century before (*i.e.*, at the time when *Elpenor* was written). Goethe then carried the material for some months in his head, until he had got far enough away from it to be able to begin on a rendering of his own. Then the sketch of the play was laid aside for some time. He was not quite pleased with it. When he took it up again, almost two years later, he discovered that, in his first treatment, he had not sufficiently studied the material of the original; it was only then that he finally gave the piece a Greek setting. In the process certain motives from the Greek legend crept in. But this mixture of elements distressed Goethe. The recasting resulted in two strata which refused to combine. Goethe perceived this, and, after a few days, gave up the task. None the less he took the piece with him to Italy to finish; it is mentioned several times in his Italian diary. In the end, however, the play was laid aside. Its place was taken by the purely classical *Iphigenie*. Later, in 1787–1788, we have to note a passage in the *Tag- und Jahresheften* according to which, at the suggestion of Herder, he was thinking of taking the subject in hand again. (The fact that it was Herder who urged him to do this may be taken as an indication that the piece was founded on an outlandish, non-European original.) Many years later, in July, 1798, Goethe happened to find the MS. of *Elpenor* again in a heap of old papers: "As I have nothing by me, having left everything behind in Jena, I have had to fall back on my old papers, and have found all sorts of things, quite sufficient to occupy us for the present."[12] He then sent the fragment to Schiller with the remark: "I don't feel inclined to look into the other enclosed MS. It may be an example of incredibly wrong handling of material and a warning against I don't know what besides. I am very curious to know what sort of a nativity you will cast for this unfortunate production." Meanwhile his Italian journey had preoccupied him entirely with the antique; his affection for Frau von Stein, which had originally kept up his interest in this work, had passed—in fact, the piece was a painful reminder to him of that time. In 1807 he wrote to Zelter that the piece was now too remote from him for him to be able to form an opinion about it. That was the end of the *Elpenor* episode.

Into the interval fall certain remarks of Goethe's which should not be passed over. In 1787 among the curiosities of the Naples Museum his attention was attracted by two pieces of Chinese work which were " both of them conceived with great naïveté and elaborately executed "; he thought them " exceptionally beautiful." Such single objects could give him pleasure, but the forms of Chinese art as a whole remained entirely foreign to him. They are at the back of his mind when in the *Italienische Reise* he decries the love of his own age for the flamboyant (*schnörkelhaft*) and the misshapen.

On the other hand, he could appreciate the minute care and conscientious work of the Chinese craftsmen. That appealed to his sense of the correct. In the *Farbenlehre* (Theory of Colour), which dates from the nineties, he says: " Yet with a lower development of culture a certain differentiation of materials and likewise a certain purity and consistency was possible, and the technique gained infinitely from tradition. It is for this reason that we find colour in such a high degree of perfection among peoples of static civilization—Egyptians, Indians, and Chinese. Static peoples put religion into their technique. Their preliminary work and preparation of materials is very conscientious and exact, the execution, stage by stage, very elaborate. They go to work with something of the slowness of Nature; and, in this way, they produce work which nations more capable of civilization and rapid progress find it impossible to imitate."[13] We shall see later on how fully Goethe appreciated in a different reference the ' static ' character of the East as contrasted with the hurried progress of the West.

Meanwhile we find another little *Chinoiserie* in the enchantment scene of the *Gross-Kophta* (1791). The scene is intended to create a weird and bizarre effect. The 'Count' makes his niece gaze into an illuminated globe standing on a mystical tripod. After some incomprehensible murmurings, the girl says: "I see tapers, bright burning tapers in a magnificent apartment. Now I distinguish Chinese tapestries, gilded carvings, a chandelier. I am dazzled by the many lights."[14] A phantom from a remote, fabulous world appears and its features are Chinese.

To this period also, about 1790, belongs a Venetian epigram which brings together Romantic sentiment and the Chinese:

> " *But what advantages me that even the Chinaman*
> *paints with laborious care Werthers and Lottes on glass ?*"*

In a similar satirical vein is the epigram *The Chinaman in Rome* of a few years later (1796):

"A Chinaman I saw in Rome ; all the buildings without an exception
ancient and modern alike seemed to him heavy and gross.
'Ah !' he exclaims with a sigh, ' Poor souls ! will they some day learn
*   that*
elegant pillars of wood are the only support for a roof,
that a compound of paper and laths and fretwork painted and gilded
gives to the liberal sense of the cultured its only delight ?'—
In him I seemed to behold how many a frivolous æsthete !
who the light webs he spins out of his brain would compare
with Nature's eternal woof, who labels the sound and the healthy
morbid, and he, the diseased, he is the only one sound !"†

But most remarkable is the occasion of this poem, namely, "an arrogant expression used by Herr Richter in a letter

---

* Doch was fördert es mich, dass auch sogar der Chinese
   Malet mit ängstlicher Hand Werthern und Lotten auf Glas ?

† Einen Chinesen sah ich in Rom: die gesamten Gebäude
   Alter und neuer Zeit schienen ihm lästig und schwer.
   Ach, so seufzt er, die Armen ! ich hoffe sie sollen begreifen
   Wie erst Säulchen von Holz tragen des Daches Gezelt,
   Dass an Latten und Pappen, Geschnitz und bunter Vergoldung
   Sich des gebildeten Augs freierer Sinn nur erfreut.—
   Siehe, da glaubt' ich im Bilde so manchen Schwärmer zu schauen,
   Der sein luftig Gespinst mit der soliden Natur
   Ewigem Teppich vergleicht, den echten reinen Gesunden
   Krank nennt, dass ja nur Er heisse, der Kranke, gesund.

to Knebel."[15] In consequence of this the long-haired
Romantic Jean Paul (Friedrich Richter) has to put up with
being likened by Goethe to a Chinaman. Schiller on receipt
of the poem wrote: " The Chinaman should go hot into
print; that is the right way to deal with these folk."[16]

Parallel with these last utterances of Goethe's runs his
perusal of two works on China, his extracts from which we
possess. One of them was *Lord Anson's Voyage Round the
World . . . in the Years* 1740–1744 (translated into German,
1749, Leipzig-Göttingen); what the other was we do not
know for certain; probably it was also a book of travels.
Works of this kind usually described only concrete observations. This is borne out by Goethe's extracts. These contain only matter of secondary importance; anyhow they could
not have given him a very high opinion of China.

We have to remember that in those days nothing of the
pantheistic mysticism of Lao Tzŭ and his disciples, which
would certainly have attracted Goethe, had been translated
in Europe. Translations from the Chinese were limited to
the classical books of Confucius. And his commonplace
philosophy made no impression on Goethe. Moreover, these
translations, compared with those of our own day, frequently misrepresented the original; so that Goethe, though
really without reason, was, as he wrote to Schiller in January,
1798, " vastly amused at the conversation between a Chinaman, who had created the external world in his own head,
and a Jesuit, who saw it reflected there !"[17]

For the light-fantastical in Chinese work, he showed more
appreciation. It pleased him as a variation and relief from
the serious business of life. He felt the same about Schiller's
enigmatical Chinese fairy-play *Turandot*, which was founded
on the like-named Italian work of Gozzi. In the *Maskenzüge*
(Processions of Masks) of 1818 Goethe writes: " After so
much serious matter it will perhaps be agreeable to conclude
with a frivolous fairy-story. Let me present to you Altoum,
the fabulous Emperor of China, and Turandot, his riddle-
loving daughter."[18] Once on an earlier occasion Goethe had
spoken of *Turandot* in these terms: " I think such pieces as
this are very necessary. They serve to remind the spectator
that the whole theatrical business is only play, and that, if
he is to gain æsthetic or, it may even be, moral profit from

it, he must raise himself above it, without losing any of the enjoyment." Or again: "Could the piece be seen in its full brilliance, it would undoubtedly produce a beautiful effect and rouse to life much that is asleep in the German nature."[19] It is in any case a fact to be noted that Goethe regarded as so valuable for the German stage this treatment of a Chinese subject from "fantastic Peking," with its "peace-loving, easy-going but melancholy emperor." It may well have reminded him of his *Elpenor*, and have made him feel that he had there attempted the impossible task of pouring Chinese material into a correct, tragic mould. Here, in *Turandot*, he must clearly have perceived how much better a light, graceful form suited it. Later on, in the last years of his life, when he essayed to create in the *Chinesisch-deutsche Jahres- und Tageszeiten* a little Chinese counterpart to the *Divan*, he had not forgotten this experience.

Meanwhile he had on two occasions occupied himself seriously with Chinese studies, namely, in the years 1813–1815 and, lastly, 1827–1828. In 1813 he wrote: "I must here mention another peculiarity of mine. When any especially terrible development threatened in the political world, I used selfishly to take refuge in what was most remote. To this I must put it down that, from my return from Karlsbad onwards, I devoted myself to a serious study of the Chinese Empire. . . ."[20] The entries in his diary are chiefly under the heading *Sinica* from October 2 to 16—*i.e.*, immediately before the battle of Leipzig. At that time Goethe read Marco Polo's *De regionibus Orientalibus*, accounts of British embassies by Barrow and Macartney, the *Recherches philosophiques sur les Egyptiens et les Chinois* of Pauw, Frederick the Great's Dutch secretary, and Martini's *Atlas Sinensis*. On November 10, he informed Knebel that he was finding the Sinologist Klaproth very useful.

Here we come for the first time upon the motive which, according to his own words, drove him to the East. He sees in the East the symbol of a quiet development. This change of attitude is an expression of the great change which was going on in Goethe's whole mind. The subjective becomes less and less prominent with the shifting of the standpoint from which he measures phenomena; he generalizes, fixes his eye upon the type, in order later to find in Law the stable point in the flux of Being, the ultimate possibility of knowledge.

But it was not only during the agitated years of the war, but also in the calmer time that followed, that Goethe, now almost seventy years old, was glad to withdraw himself into the serene world of the East. In his notice of Rückert's *Oestliche Rosen* (Roses of the East) he writes: " But now that peace has come at last, and a man can hope, if only for a few short hours, to enjoy with a light heart converse with cheerful society, a breath of outlandish air to cool and refresh us, like an East wind, is not unwelcome."[21]

The Goethe of these years has already sufficiently extricated himself from his materials to be able to survey the field and to take comprehensive views. In place of tracing lines of descent in the history of developments we now find him rather drawing parallels and comparisons. The gathering of his life's harvest has to some extent already begun. This changed point of view naturally makes itself felt even within our limited field. A note of the year 1808 runs: " Among other remarkable possessions he had an old Chinese carpet with separate figures combined by means of a suitable ground into a complete design. I remembered to have seen something like it, dating from early German times, in the cathedral at Magdeburg."[22] Involuntarily Goethe here again couples Chinese with Gothic. He was probably quite unconscious that the work he had seen in the cathedral at Magdeburg was of Gothic origin. He had merely an impression of the style. A remark of a later date seems to show that in the interval he had obtained an insight into the style of Chinese draughtsmanship. In the essays on art (*Blumenmalerei*) of 1818 he says of the drawings of the botanist, Ferdinand Bauer: " Every colour, even the lightest, is darker than the white paper on which it is laid, and so neither light nor shade is needed; the parts stand out sufficiently from one another and from the background; and yet there would be something Chinese about this kind of representation, if the artist disregarded light and shade out of ignorance, instead of knowingly avoiding both as he does here."[23] Goethe is mistaken, of course, in taxing the Chinese with ignorance, but that need not trouble us for the moment. The point to be noticed is that he had discovered a law of Chinese art, though here he only alludes to it in passing—namely, its disregard of light and shade.

In our account of Goethe's Chinese studies we omitted to notice a little remark of Wilhelm Grimm. In October, 1815, he wrote to his brother: "Goethe is reading and annotating the *Hao-ch'iu-chuan*." This tale we have already come across; in 1796, Schiller spoke to Goethe about a Chinese tale, which he intended later to work upon himself.

On September 4, 1817, Goethe read a Chinese play in the English translation of Davis: *Lao-sheng-erh, An Heir in His Old Age*. He sent it to Knebel, remarking at the same time on the not very attractive impression it made at first reading; but adding that, on nearer acquaintance, he felt it to be a remarkable work.

Biedermann conjectures that the studies of these years, by which Goethe was led to pay special attention, among other things, to the almost religious importance of marks of respect among the Chinese, may have influenced the composition of the *Pädagogische Provinz*. Whether he is right I cannot say; but it is worth recording that, before I had read Biedermann's essay, the same idea had occurred to me on reading the *Pädagogische Provinz*. Goethe once, in 1821, referred to Chinese ceremonial as typical of their civilization as contrasted with that of the West. In his essay on *Indian and Chinese Poetry*, he writes that the Chinese drama, with which he had recently made acquaintance, "is very reminiscent of Iffland's *Hagestolz*, except that, with the Germans, the atmosphere or the oddities of domestic and civil surroundings could furnish all that was required, while with the Chinese, in addition to these motives, religious and civic ceremonial make their contribution." (The generalizations should be noted.)[24]

As we are now in the region of the *Wanderjahre*, we must not forget to mention a little *Chinoiserie* which is to be found there. "His chief endeavour," Goethe writes, "was now to find his way out of the park into the open country and on to the road which was to lead him to his friend. He was hesitating as to the direction, when on his left, projecting above the bushes, on a strange kind of scaffolding, his eye fell upon the hermitage, about which they had made such a mystery; and yet now to his great astonishment, on the gallery under the Chinese roof, he beheld the good old man, who for some days had been supposed to be sick, gazing cheerfully about him."[25] It was no accident that made Goethe give his wonderful old man a Chinese hut for a dwelling. This figure of the long-haired old master with a turn for solitude reminded him of the forms of the old Chinese sages met with in the pages of Du Halde and elsewhere.

But from all this, it must not by any means be inferred that Goethe was personally touched by the ' China-mania ' of the eighteenth century. We have several remarks from him which make this quite clear. In the *Campagne in Frankreich* he comes to speak of the sceptical times of Voltaire, and in this connexion mentions Pauw, the secretary of Frederick the Great, of whom we have several times had occasion to speak: " Thus De Pauw directed his conquering glance upon more distant continents; he would not allow either to the Chinese or to the Egyptians the honours which a prejudice of many years' growth had heaped upon them."[26]

In the treatise on *Modern German Religious and Patriotic Art* (Writings, 1816–1832), in which, it is true, Heinrich Meyer also had a hand, Goethe says: " There are artistic as well as technical, ethical and mechanical reasons why it is quite impossible to transpose oneself completely into the spirit of past times, to get their essence from them. . . . If examples are needed, we would point to a highly cultured neighbouring people, who, fifty years ago, were equally unsuccessful in imitating the curious taste of the Chinese in buildings and pictures."[27] He refers, of course, to the French.

In the papers *Zur Morphologie* among the *Maximen und Reflexionen* (1822) his unprejudiced view of China is clearly expressed: " May the study of Roman and Greek literature ever remain the basis of our higher education; . . . Chinese, Indian, Egyptian antiquities are nothing more than curiosities; it is good to make oneself and the world acquainted with them, but they will contribute little to our moral and æsthetic education."[28] This was not in the least meant as a judgment of value; it merely stated that here two essentially different worlds are confronted—in China a world completed and a world becoming in the West. The East had for

Goethe a symbolical character, and, as such, instructional importance. This point of view emerges more and more clearly. It is very characteristically and covertly expressed in some lines in the second part of *Faust*, which we quote here with some hesitation. Wagner and Mephistopheles are in the laboratory. Wagner speaks (turning to the fireplace):

> " *What once we deemed the mysteries of Nature*
> *Our probing wit dares now to analyze ;*
> *And what we once admired as organism*
> *We now dissect, dissolve and crystallize.*

> MEPHISTOPHELES :
> *He who lives long, sees many things ;*
> *For him in this world nothing new can be.*
> *In former days, when I was on my travels,*
> *I have seen crystallized humanity.*"[29]*

' Crystallized humanity ' no doubt means the Chinese, in whom, therefore, Goethe has seen not a dead, formless mass, but the representatives of a form no longer, indeed, capable of further development, but simply crystallized. For the aged Goethe, this was an image not altogether unrelated to the condition which he had himself reached.

And in these years he again essayed to cast into his own mould Chinese material. The result was the *Chinesisch-deutsche Jahres- und Tageszeiten*. For this, as for *Elpenor*, Biedermann has made a useful study of sources.[30] We need therefore treat of it only briefly.

Among Goethe's posthumous poems are some translations from a Chinese collection, the *Hundred Poems of Beautiful Women* (*Po Meï Hsin Yung*). At the head of the paper is written: " The loveliest woman—February 2, 1826—Chinese."[31] In the literary essays is a dissertation: *Chinese matter—relating to the poems of a hundred beautiful women.*

* WAGNER :
> Was man an der Natur geheimnisvolles pries, .
> Das wagen wir verständig zu probieren,
> Und was sich sonst organisieren liess,
> Das lassen wir kistallisieren.

MEPHISTOPHELES :
> Wer lange lebt, hat viel erfahren,
> Nichts neues kann fur ihn auf dieser Welt geschehn.
> Ich habe schon in meinen Wanderjahren
> Kristallisiertes Menschenvolk gesehen.

They " give us the conviction," says Goethe, " that, in spite
of all limitations, people could still live and love and write
poetry in that curious and remarkable empire."[32] These
Chinese poems must have inspired him once more to occupy
himself seriously with Chinese literature; for from February
to August of the year 1827 we find in the diaries a whole
series of entries which point to this. On February 2nd and
3rd he reads a ' Chinese Poem,' *Chinese Courtship ;* on
February 5th, the entry is ' Chinese Poetesses '; on May 14th
and 19th, ' The Chinese Tale translated by Rémusat '[33]; on
August 22nd, ' *Contes Chinois* continued.' [34] Last and not
least, Goethe must have read at that time the Chinese idyll
Hua Ch'ien Chi (The Story of the ' Flower-paper'). For he
tells Eckermann in reference to a Chinese story on January
31st: " One hears all the time the goldfish plashing in the
pools; the birds sing unceasingly in the branches, the day
is always bright and sunny, the night always clear; the moon
is often spoken of, but it makes no difference to the landscape, its light is for them as bright as the day itself. Such
conditions can only have been found in the *Flower-paper*.
The inference is not invalidated by the fact that some of
the things described by Goethe do not occur in the *Flower-
paper ;* for example, the story of the youth and the girl who
spend a night together without moving. That Goethe took
from another story, which appeared, in 1820, in an English
translation as *The Affectionate Pair,* and of which, in 1853,
Kurz made a version with the title of *The Male and Female
Brother.* Certain it is in any case that a whole series of
motives, about which he told Eckermann, were taken by
Goethe from the *Flower-paper.* He becomes quite excited
over the telling: " I heard the lovely maidens laughing,
and when I came in sight of them, they were sitting on rush
chairs. There you have at once the most charming situation,
for rush chairs are inseparable in thought from the utmost
degree of lightness and daintiness. And now a number of
legends. . . ." Light, dainty, sketchy, " charming situation "—the phrases describe the happily chosen style of
the *Chinesisch-deutsche Jahres- und Tageszeiten.* Never did
Goethe express himself at such length on a single Chinese
work as on the tale above mentioned. For that reason
Biedermann is doubtless right in giving the *Flower-paper*

as the essential source of the *Chinesisch-deutsche Jahres- und Tageszeiten*. In both, there is the same general vaporous atmosphere, the same delicacy of natural feeling, the same brilliant moon, the like mood of a happy summer's day.

The *Chinesisch-deutsche Jahres- und Tageszeiten* were no copy; that was not Goethe's manner of handling foreign material. He gives it the impress of his own nature; it is only rarely that any indication remains of the original source, as for instance when he speaks of the " town in the North," meaning Peking. It is only the foreign spirit of the original which is faithfully preserved, and even that he makes genuinely his own. The music of these delightful little poems is like " the splashing of goldfish," like the music in the air of a " bright and sunny " day; the impression made by the verse is " clean and delicate " as the carvings from that far-distant land; it is as if behind the lines the " laughter " of those " lovely maidens " could be heard, lightly and daintily echoed in the quiet rhythm of the verse. Goethe has here reproduced with a real happiness of touch the deep happiness of spirit which he felt in the Far East. Small and unpretentious in form, as befitted the Chinese, but complete and exhaustive.

The work represented perfectly the general impression made on him by the Chinese during the last years of his life. Everything belonging to that world seemed to him light, delicate, almost ethereal, the relations of things cleanly and clearly defined, the inner and the outer life serene and free from convulsions, something like battledore and shuttlecock perfectly played, without a single clumsy movement; as if there both outer and inner life ran on noiselessly on age-old lines of traditional law.

Just as Goethe speaks of the " lightness and delicacy " of Chinese outdoor life, he coins the phrase " of almost super-Chinese lightness " in reference to architecture.[35] And of the moral sense of the Chinese he says: " Only that with them life is clearer, purer, more moral; they everywhere appear as sensible folk, good citizens, without much passion or poetic fervour; and in this they bear a strong resemblance to my *Hermann and Dorothea*, as also to the English novels of Richardson." (*Conversation with Eckermann*, October 31st, 1827.) He speaks in the same way of the legends, "which all run on morality and propriety." And all the sanity of his wise old age is in the words: " But it is this strict moderation in all things which has preserved the Chinese Empire for thousands of years and will continue to preserve it." There was something in the outlook of his old age which drew him to these characteristics of the East; his feeling for law, for the safe road, the *Tao* of the Chinese. The calm and balanced quality in Chinese public morality attracted the aged Goethe, as the restless, complicated impression produced by their art had repelled him as a youth. The comprehensive view of old age joyfully included this Oriental world in its scope: " I see more and more," he said to Eckermann on that 31st of January, 1827, " that poetry is a common possession of mankind. . . . The expression ' National literature ' does not mean much now, the age of ' world-literature ' is at hand, and everyone should endeavour to hasten its coming." And China, we see, contributed something to this favourite thought of his last years. Greek is, of course, still the standard, but the non-European has also a certain value of its own as a means to culture.

If now we examine our gains: our enquiry has certainly added nothing of any real value to our general conception of Goethe; but in the course of it we have gained one thing—a sharpened perception of the universal and the significant in little, disconnected facts. A single ripple in the stream of human life seems at first to be merely an unrelated single ripple, but, if we look more closely, we discover that in reality it is borne forward by the one great stream, of which it is the miniature image, one among the many.

LAST WORDS

LAST WORDS

In Goethe the relation of Europe to the East reached its maturity. With him, then, our work comes to a natural conclusion. The few words here added are merely intended to explain how it was that the very period covered by Goethe's life coincided with a decline—of course only in the spiritual sense—of European relations with the East.

The beginning of the eighteenth century had been celebrated by the French court, in innocent ignorance of what the century had in store, with splendid masquerades ' à la chinoise.' The Rococo had been fertilized with the rich artistic treasures of Southern China; the Enlightenment had called to its aid the severe, matter-of-fact, ' rational ' North Chinese, Confucius; the Physiocrats had taken their theory of the economic basis of the State mainly from the conditions of ancient China; and finally the great ' back-to-Nature ' reaction, as it degenerated into sentimental Nature-worship, seized upon the Chinese garden as the temple of its over-refined cult of Feeling. This took place in the seventh and eighth decades of the century, and heralded the approaching end of that close connexion of Europe with China which had lasted for almost a century. The reasons for this falling off of interest are manifold. We will try to pick out some of them.

In the seventeenth and eighteenth centuries, the Jesuits formed the link connecting the mind of Europe with the Far East. But their activities in China were, after 1723, very much curtailed in consequence of the unhappy controversy which took place over ritual. The Chinese, in view of the disputes between the various Catholic orders, then began to regard Christians as apostles of discord, and commenced persecutions, which, even in the eyes of the missionaries, obscured the fair image of ancient China. The missionaries began to blame, where before they had only praised. If we compare the *Mémoires concernant l'histoire, etc., de la Chine* (a new series of letters from Chinese Jesuits beginning in 1776) with the *Lettres édifiantes et curieuses*, which had appeared fifty years earlier, we are, on the whole, surprised by their matter-of-fact, impartial judgments, in which blame is mingled with praise and a certain bitterness of tone makes itself felt. Then came the decay of Jesuit influence in Europe, following on the official dissolution of the Order in France in 1762, which was made complete in 1773. But every injury done to the Order also affected the spiritual relations of the West with the East. The unfavourable judgments of the commercial circles gained at the same time a wider hearing. Doubt having once become strong, opinions which had been hardening for a hundred years ventured to express themselves.

De Guignes, as a scientist, cast doubt on the veracity of the Chinese annals,[1] which for a century past had been so much admired. From England came a crushing condemnation of Chinese philosophy itself: it had never got beyond a stage so primitive that it was not worth while occupying oneself with it.[2]

The breaking off of intellectual relations with the East proceeded the more rapidly as economic interests thrust themselves almost exclusively into the foreground. The spirit of the nineteenth century is already announcing itself. For example, the eleventh volume of the *Mémoires concernant l'histoire, etc.* (1786), contains little else but reports on the occurrence of minerals and other things of importance to industry in China, such as borax, lignite, quicksilver, ammoniac, and bamboos, or on horses, wool-bearing animals, and so forth. The idea of China as, above all, a first-rate world-market is beginning to be the sole concern of public opinion. This development was accentuated by the fact that in the second half of the century England was steadily and persistently tending to monopolize relations with China. English literature on China came to occupy itself more and more with purely practical and commercial interests. *The Chinese Traveller* of 1775 is a typical instance.[3] From 1785 onwards, topographical descriptions and atlases were multiplied; efforts were presently made also to interest the youth of England in the Far East. In 1817 appeared *The Traveller in Asia, or a Visit to the Most Celebrated Parts*

of the East Indies and China, for the Instruction and Enter-
tainment of Young Persons.[4]

In France the intellectual interest survived longer, at
least among lovers of art. But about the middle of the
nineteenth century the Sinologist G. Pauthier complained
that there also the Chinese questions, which in the time of
Leibniz had so keenly interested the philosophic and religious worlds, "now scarcely attracted the attention of a
select few." "These people, whom we daily treat as barbarians, and who, nevertheless, had attained to a very high
state of culture several centuries before our ancestors in-
habited the forests of Gaul and Germany, now inspire in us
only a deep contempt."[5]

Then there was the fact that another world was rising
again from its ruins—the world of ancient Greece and Rome.
Its emergence in the seventies of last century coincided in
time with the decay of relations with the East. Plutarch
began to displace Confucius. A general change of orientation followed. People even essayed to find the origins of
Chinese culture in ancient Greece. Christoph Meiners,
professor of philosophy in Göttingen, wrote in 1778: " This
contact of the Chinese of the *Han* dynasty, in the latter half
of the second century, with the intellectually advanced inhabitants and conquerors of Sogdiana and Bactria, and the
consequent transference of Greek knowledge and culture to
China, is not only made highly probable, but is placed almost
beyond doubt by trustworthy historical data."[6] In Meiners'
opinion it will no longer be doubted " that the people who
really shed light upon the dark places of the earth, the Greeks,
had illuminated Eastern Asia even earlier than Western and
Northern Europe."[7]

In particular he thinks that the Arabs, " soon after they
had been placed by the Abbassids in possession of almost
all the treasures of Greek wisdom," successfully disseminated
these among the Chinese.[8]

This was the general view, in face of which little importance attaches to the attempt of Joseph Hager, in a work
dating from the last years of the eighteenth century, to prove
the precise opposite—namely, that the old Greek worship,
along with its sacrificial instruments, had come to the West
from China.[9]

Generally the rôles were exchanged. As in the beginning of the century China had been held to be the original birthplace of human wisdom, so now, as the century neared its close, the Greeks were exalted as the greatest teachers of mankind. "How can you believe that uncultivated Oriental peoples produced annals and poetry and possessed a complete religion and morality, before the Greeks, who were the teachers of Europe, were able to read ? How can you think it possible that nations of this kind, so many centuries before Alexander, should have expressed themselves in these books with a sublimity, a truthfulness, a nobility, an eloquence, a majesty, such as is scarcely to be found in Roman masterpieces, and which, in respect of religious, moral and philosophical ideas, raise them, Holy Writ excepted, to the very first rank ?"[10] If the former boundless admiration of China was to be regarded as grotesque, this uncritical contempt was no less so.

In matters of art the change was naturally no less apparent. A group in Berlin porcelain by Gottfried Schadow expresses it in satirical fashion. The piece bears the title: *Triumph of Antique Architecture over the Rococo*.[11] The excavations at Pompeii and Herculaneum brought to light a number of Roman and Greek ornaments, which were soon made familiar to the world in volumes of drawings and engravings. People soon ran into as great extravagances as had the men of the Rococo, and had to endure like ridicule. We may mention the *Mascarade à la grecque*—caricatures published in Parma in 1771 by E. A. Petitot.[12] In less than a generation the reaction had begun. We discussed the Rococo painter, Boucher, as an example of the Louis XV style; his son, Juste François Boucher, in his engravings of about the year 1775, already exhibits the severe style of Louis XVI. Even in the development of the sense for colour the change is clearly seen. While the Rococo had been fond of delicate colours, the preference now was either for monochrome or for very bright, striking colours. The Rococo had educated the sense for even the most delicate gradations, the new middle-class society demanded simpler and more downright sensations. Colour was either completely renounced, so that, for instance, in the decoration of interiors, the place of gilding was taken by a curiously unassuming light grey; or else people intoxicated themselves with strong colours; thus the delicately tinted Chinese silks gave place to Indian materials, whose gaudiness would formerly have been offensive, but which now were largely in demand.

Presently Indian culture generally invaded the field of European taste; Indian Mysticism ousted Chinese Illumination, and played in the nineteenth century a part similar to, if less noticeable than, that which the latter had played a century before.[13]

NOTES

NOTES

BRIEF REVIEW OF THE CONTACTS BETWEEN EUROPE AND CHINA UP TO THE END OF THE EIGHTEENTH CENTURY.

[1] Fr. Hirth, *China and the Roman Orient: Researches into their Ancient and Medieval Relations as represented in old Chinese Records*, Leipzig and Munich, 1885.

Fr. Hirth, *Chinesische Studien*, Leipzig, 1890, pp. 1-24.

Fr. von Richthofen, *Über die zentralasiatischen Handelsstrassen bis zum 2. Jahrhundert nach Christus*, Berlin, 1877, p. 96 ff.

H. Nissen, *Der Verkehr zwischen China und dem römischen Reiche* (*Jahrbücher des Vereins von Altertumsfreunden im Rheinlande*, xlv), Bonn, 1894.

Albert Hermann, *Die alten Seidenstrassen zwischen China und Syrien*, Berlin, 1910.

[2] Marco Polo, in the *Bibliothek berühmter Reisen*.

[3] Noël, '*Histoire du commerce du monde*,' Paris, 1894, ii, p. 161.

[4] The voyage from Amsterdam to China and back in the seventeenth century still took from two to three years. (The Company could, for example, only fit out thirteen trips between 1611 and 1634.) Later, in the eighteenth century, the double journey could be made in one and a half years. The tonnage of the vessels on the China route averaged at the beginning of the seventeenth century three hundred tons, at the end of the seventeenth century the English were already employing 1,100-ton ships, and in the eighteenth century the tonnage rose to 1,500. (Noël, l.c., p. 88; Henri Cordier, *La France en Chine*, p. 200.)

[5] With this the figures given by Savary, *Dictionnaire Universel*, v (especially 1610–1612), agree.

[6] Noël, l.c., ii, p. 162.

[7] Savary, l.c., v (especially 1615–1623).

[8] Savary, l.c., v (especially 1622).

[9] Voltaire, *Œuvres complètes*, Gotha, 1786, xxxvii, p. 508.

[10] Noël, l.c., ii, p. 324.

[11] *Sendschreiben aus den weitberümten Landschaften u.s.w.*, Dillingen, 1589, p. 23.

[12] *Sendschreiben*, p. 27.

[13] *ibid.*, p. 19.

[14] The widely-circulated story of the porcelain, which had to remain buried in the earth one hundred years in order to harden, is told as follows in the *Embarras de la Foire de Beaucaire en vers burlesque* (1716):

> " *Allons à cette porcelaine*
> *Sa beauté m'invite, m'entraîne,*
> *Elle vient du monde nouveau,*
> *L'on ne peut rien voir de plus beau,*
> *Qu'elle a d'attrait et qu'elle est fine!*
> *Elle est native de la Chine.*
> *La terre avait au moins cent ans*
> *Que fit des vases si galants . . .*
> *Outre leur attrait divin*
> *Ils ne souffrent point le venin . . .*
> *Et semblent s'ouvrir de douleur*
> *Du crime de l'empoisonneur.*"

[15] Belevitch-Stankevitch, *La Chine en France au temps de Louis XIV*, Paris, 1910, p. 241.

[16] *La Chine d'Athanase Kircher de la Société de Jésus, illustrée de plusieurs monuments, etc.*, Amsterdam, 1670. A translation of *China monumentis qua sacris qua profanis illustrata*, second ed., 1667, Amsterdam.

[17] *Monumenti sinici quod anno domini CICICCXXV terris in ipsa China erutum . . . lectis versio, translatio . . . P. Athan-Kircherus . . . edidit tonos vocibus addidit, etc.*

[18] éd. Astié, second ed., p. 523.

[19] *Confucius Sinarum philosophus, etc. . . . Prosperi Intorcetta, Christiane Herdtrich, Francisci Rougimont, Philippi Couplet*, Paris, 1687.

[20] Louis Le Comte, *Das heutige Sina* (from the French), Frankfurt a. M. and Leipzig, 1699, i, p. 309.

[21] Belevitch-Stankevitch, l.c., p. 20.

[22] Preface by Justi to *Vergleichung der europäischen mit den asiatischen u.a. vermeintlich barbarischen Regierungen*, Berlin, 1762.

[23] *Réponse à des attaques faites par M. de Sommerat contre les missionaires de la Chine;* reproduced in *Lettres édifiantes et curieuses concernant l'Asie, l'Afrique et l'Amérique*, published 1843, by the *Société du Panthéon Littéraire* in Paris, iv, p. 509.

ROCOCO.

[1] Le Comte, l.c., i., p. 221 ff.

[2] Paul Schumann, *Barock und Rokoko, Beiträge zur Kunstgeschichte*, N.F. i, p. 51 ff.

[3] Schumann, l.c., p. 50.

[4] Edition of 1761, Copenhagen, iii (especially p. 99).

[5] F. Laske, *Der ostasiatische Einfluss auf die Baukunst des Abendlandes*, Berlin, 1909, p. 69.

[6] Frederick the Great, incited by the successes of Meissen, had acquired for the sum of 225,000 Reichsthaler the porcelain factory of the merchant Gotzkowski in Berlin (afterwards the Royal Porcelain-Manufacture), Laske, l.c., p. 69.

[7] Springer, *Bilder aus der neueren Kunstgeschichte*, ii, pp. 230-231.

[8] *Embarras de la Foire de Beaucaire en vers burlesque*, 1716, Belevitch-Stankevitch, l.c., p. 150.

[9] Belevitch-Stankevitch, l.c., pp. 81-144.

[10] Mirabeau, *Ami des hommes*.
Voltaire on the other hand was an enthusiastic admirer of lacquer. In *Les Tu et les Vous* he expressed his pleasure in this latest achievement of French industry:

> " *Et les cabinets où Martin*
> *A surpassé l'art de la Chine.*"

Or in the *Premier discours de l'inégalité des conditions:*

> " *Damis courant de belle en belle*
> *Sous des lambris dorés et vernis par Martin.*"

[11] *Histoire générale des Arts appliqués à l'industrie par E. Molinier*, iii, p. 114.

[12] This and the following facts about sedan-chairs are mainly taken from *Abhandlung der Porte-Chaises oder Tragesänften durch Menschen und Thiere*, by Karl Chr. Schramm, Nürnberg, 1737.

[13] Schramm, l.c.

[14] As the English called porcelain ' China ' after the land of its origin, so they gave to the imitations of lacquer the name ' Japanning,' because most of the lacquer came from Japan.

[15] The officials of the Trading Company ' earned ' indirectly enormous fortunes. For instance, the Governor-General of the Dutch Company, Wackenier, brought home from his four years' residence in Batavia (1737–1741) a fortune of five million florins. (Noël, l.c., p. 162; Belevitch-Stankevitch, l.c., p. 189.)

[16] Savary, l.c., v (especially 1203).

[17] Savary, l.c. (especially 1261).

[18] von Schorn, *Die Textilkunst*, Leipzig-Prag, 1885, p. 193.

[19] Belevitch-Stankevitch, l.c., p. 193.

[20] April, 1673.

[21] Belevitch-Stankevitch, l.c., p. 195.

[22] This was true—according to Savary—even of the second half of the eighteenth century.

[23] Henri Cordier, *La Chine en France au XVIIIme siècle*, Paris, 1910, pp. 48, 49.

[24] Belevitch-Stankevitch, l.c., p. 201.

[25] Foundation of the *Compagnie des Indes Orientales*.

[26] Belevitch-Stankevitch, l.c., p. 198.

[27] *ibid.*, p. 190.

[28] *ibid.*, p. 206.

[29] *ibid.*, p. 210.

[30] But had no further practical importance.

[31] Savary, *Dictionnaire universel*, ii (especially p. 214).

[32] Of a more general influence of the Rococo there can be no question except in Piedmont, the borderland; see Dreger, *Die künstlerische Entwicklung der Weberei und Stickerei*, Vienna, 1904, p. 291.

[33] Dreger, l.c., p. 278, and plates 311b and c. Particularly fine specimens also in the collection of textiles in the East Asiatic Museum at Cologne.

[34] Charpentier-Cossigny, *Voyage à Canton*, 1699, pp. 419 and 474.

[35] Merck's *Warenlexikon*, sixth ed., Leipzig, 1919; see the articles on the subject.

[36] Dreger, l.c., p. 285 ff.

[37] See the Reproductions of them in Dreger, l.c., ii, 295c.

[38] G. Macon, *Les arts dans la Maison de Condé*, *Revue de l'Art*, xi, 1902, p. 206.

[39] See, for example, Dreger, l.c., ii, p. 290 (half-length figure).

[40] Dreger, l.c., i, p. 302.

[41] ii, 399, No. 1443.

[42] ii, 459, No. 2000; 122, No. 268.

[43] Dreger, l.c., i, p. 264.

[44] Before this there had been, in the sixteenth century, a general rise in the cost of living; after 1618, the Thirty Years' War had a like effect. The consequence was the rapid impoverishment of Germany.

[45] Obviously a case of Chinese influence.

[46] These two German brothers discovered a special process for the finer hangings. The pattern was drawn on a groundwork of dull varnished colours. Gold and silver was then stamped on to it by means of engraved plates of copper. It is possible that they brought the secret with them from Germany, for in the already mentioned note of Jean Papillon there is a remark to the effect that the German hangings of 1638 were printed with heated copper-plates, engraved in the same way as for black and white etching.

[47] In order to avoid English importation there was issued in 1753 an order forbidding the importation of "*papier drapé à usage de tapisserie.*"

[48] Grimm, *Correspondance littéraire*, 15th May, 1756.

[49] Newhof, *L'Ambassade vers l'Empereur de la Chine*, French ed., 1665. Quoted by Belevitch-Stankevitch, p. 177.

[50] Belevitch-Stankevitch, l.c., p. 177.

[51] Le Comte, l.c., i, p. 225.

[52] *L'œuvre d'Antoine Watteau d'après des dessins originaux*, Paris (Book of plates; no date).

[53] Maugras, *La Cour de Lunéville*, Paris, 1904, p. 108.

[54] Adolf Rosenberg, *Antoine Watteau*, Leipzig, 1896, p. 17.

[55] Belevitch-Stankevitch, l.c., p. 243.

[56] A. Watteau, Paris, 1892, p. 32 ff.

[57] Okakuro Kakuzo, *Das Buch vom Tee*. From the English. Leipzig, Inselverlag, p. 50.

[58] *Cahier de six Baraques Chinoises, inventées et dessinées par Jean Pillement, premier peintre du roi de Pologne.*

[59] Raymond Koechlin, *La Chine en France au XVIIIme siècle*, in *Gazette des Beaux Arts*, p. 98. This article describes certain ' chinoi-series ' from the exhibition which was opened at the time under this title at the *Musée des Arts décoratifs*.

[60] Koechlin, l.c., p. 100.

[61] *ibid.*, p. 101.

[62] Dreger, l.c., p. 257.

[63] The German originals are mostly to be found in the excellent collection of ornamental embroidery in the *Kunstgewerbe Museum* of Berlin.

[64] *Mémoires de Bertin*, unpublished MS. in the *Bibliothèque de l'Institut* (see H. Cordier, l.c., pp. 56-58).

[65] *Traité du beau essentiel dans les Arts, appliqué particulièrement à l'Architecture*, 1752, and *L'art de bâtir des Maisons de Campagne*, 1743.

[66] *Nouveau Traité de toute l'Architecture.*

[67] *Nouveaux mémoires sur l'état présent de la Chine*, i, p. 130 ff.

[68] *Lettres édifiantes et curieuses*, Paris, 1843, iii, p. 791.

[69] *ibid.*, p. 791.

[70] *ibid.*, p. 787.

[71] E. Molinier, *Histoire Générale des Arts appliqués à l'Industrie*, p. 323.

[72] Jeanne Bouché, *Servandoni*, *Gazette des Beaux Arts*, 1910, pp. 121-146.

[73] P. Attiret, *Lettres édifiantes et curieuses*, Paris, 1843, iii, p. 791.

[74] H. Cordier, l.c., p. 84.

[75] Belevitch-Stankevitch, l.c., p. 100.

[76] Marie-Luise Gothein, *Die Geschichte der Gartenkunst*, Jena, 1914, ii, p. 217.

[77] Reproductions, see Jolles, *Altholland*, p. 154 ff.

[78] Reproductions in F. Laske, *Der ostasiatische Einfluss auf die Baukunst des Abendlandes, vornehmlich Deutschland, im XVIII. Jahrhundert*, Berlin, 1909, p. 83.

[79] We find a pleasing explanation of these earliest middle-class country-houses in *Oud-Nederlandsche Tuinkunst door van Sypesteyn*, 's Gravenhage, 1910.

[80] Fritz Hirsch, *Das Bruchsaler Schloss*, Heidelburg, 1910 (Picture-book).

[81] Cordier, l.c., pp. 67-78.

[82] Laske, l.c., p. 93.

[83] Fritz Hirsch, l.c.

[84] Gothelin, l.c., ii, 226 and Illustration.

[85] Baltzer, *Kulturbauten Japans*, p. 13.

[86] Laske, l.c., p. 41.

[87] Laske, l.c., p. 47.   The reader should remember also Menzel's painting of the Round Table at Sans-Souci.

[88] *ibid.*, Illustrations 36 and 37, p. 33.

[89] Belevitch-Stankevitch, l.c., p. 178.

[90] *Encyclopédie*, éd. 1780, xiii, p. 72.

[91] Albert Ilg, *Die Fischer von Erlach*, Vienna, 1896.

[92] Cordier, l.c., pp. 81-93.

[93] *ibid.*, p. 87 ff.

[94] La Grand d'Aussy, *Histoire de la vie privée des François*, ed. 1815, ii, p. 73.

[95] *Spectacles des Foires et des Boulevards de Paris*, 1776, p. 117; Grimm, l.c., August 15th, 1770; Magine, *Histoire des Marionettes*, p. 150.

[96] From the number of Comedies and Music-plays popular at that date we may mention the following: *Les Chinois*, comedy in five Acts, came out in the collection: *Le Théâtre Italien de Gherardi*, Paris, 1700, v, pp. 211-278; *Il Cinese Rimpatriato, divertimento scenico, da rapresentarsi in Parigi, nel Teatro dell' Opera*, 1753; *Ces Chinois*, comedy in one Act, verse interspersed with songs, a parody of *Il Cinese Rimpatriato*; *Le Chinois de Retour*, lyrical scene, first performed 1753, in the Opera House at Paris; *Le Chinois Poli en France*, parody of the *Chinois de Retour*, in one Act, Paris, 1754; *Le Ballet chinois et turc*, 1755; *Les Tartares*, Ballet, 1755; *La Rencontre imprévue*, 1764; *La Matrone chinoise*, 1765; *La fête chinoise*, Ballet, 1778; *L'idolo Cinese*, 1779.

[97] The piece was never printed.   The MS. is in the National Library in Paris, MS. No. 9,314 and 25,471.

[98] Three Acts, Collection *Théâtre de la Foire*, vol. viii, Paris, 1731.

[99] *Il Cinese Rimpatriato*, 1753; *Le Chinois poli*, 1754; *Les Chinois*, 1756.

[100] Belevitch-Stankevitch, l.c., pp. 81-144.

[101] Laske, l.c., p. 57.

[102] Muthesius, *Das englische Haus*, iii, p. 84.

THE AGE OF ENLIGHTENMENT.

[1] In the eighteenth century the influence of Turkish motives is almost entirely limited to erotic literature (Letters from the Harem).   In France, where reaction to exotic influences was most lively, subjects were taken by preference from the Turkish.   *Turqueries*—in the second half of the seventeenth century—formed the first phase of a markedly exotic literature in France.   Especially fertile were the years 1770–1785.   During that period were produced twenty Turkish histories, ten Turkish romances, five pieces for the stage.

[2] *Description de l'Empire Chinois*, 1785, tome i, Préface, p. v.

[3] *Relation du banissement des Jésuites de la Chine*, 1769, p. 1.

[4] P. Entrecolles, *Lettres édifiantes*, éd. 1838, iii, p. 298.   October, 19, 1720.

[5] Clerc, *Yu le Grand, histoire chinoise*, 1769, p. xiii.

[6] Franz Rudolf Merkel, *Leibniz und die Chinamission*, Leipzig, 1920, p. 28.

[7] l.c., p. 29.

[8] The reference is to *Confucius Sinarum Philosophus*; see Chr. v. Rommel, *Leibniz und Landgraf Ernst von Hessen-Rheinfeld*, 1847, p. 113 ff.

[9] Merkel, l.c., p. 25.

M

[10] " So absolute is their obedience to those who are set over them, so great their respect for age, so deep the reverence of children for parents, that any violence, even of language, is an unheard-of thing, and to them seems as great a crime as patricide does to us."

[11] Liebniz' works, edited by Klopp, 1864, i, 112.

[12] Adolf Harnack, *Geschichte der preussischen Akademie*, i, first half, p. 30, note.

[13] In a memorandum addressed to the Elector, he says: " To which (*i.e.*, the Mission) now, by special disposition of Providence, the unusually good personal relations established with the Czar open a wide door into great Tartary and glorious China. By this means a *commercium* not only of wares and manufactures but of light and wisdom with this, as it were, other civilized world and Europe may find entrance." (Harnack, l.c., p. 82.)

[14] Harnack, l.c., i, 74.

[15] *ibid.*, 88.

[16] *ibid.*, 96.

[17] *ibid.*, 128 ff.

[18] See his Dissertation *De arte combinatoria*, 1666.

[19] H. Hoffmann, *Die Leibnizsche Religionsphilosophie in ihrer geschichtlichen Stellung*, 1903, p. 14 ff.

[20] de Harlez, *Le Yi-Ching*, Paris, 1897.

[21] Merkel, l.c., p. 44, note.

[22] l.c., p. 43, note.

[23] l.c., p. 44, note.

[24] He once called K'ang Hsi a " *Princeps fere sine exemplo egregius.*" (Merkel, p. 43.)

[25] See Fischer's above-mentioned *Biography Frisch.*

[26] Harnack, l.c., i, 164.

[27] For Liebniz' scheme of a Society, further details in Harnack on the contents of the *Novissima Sinica;* good general account in Merkel, l.c., pp. 37-57.

[28] Merkel, l.c., p. 54 ff.

[29] In this connexion it may also be noted that Leibniz not only wished to open up for Prussia the trans-Siberian route to China, but also recommended France to construct the Suez Canal, in order to secure for herself the shortest sea-route to the Far East. Just at that time—the end of the seventeenth century—France was endeavouring to secure an overland route through Russia, and Leibniz was naturally anxious to divert her from this.

[30] A. H. Francke, Halle, 1880.

[31] The address was printed at Frankfurt a. M. in 1726 in Latin. German version in vol. vi of the edition of Wolff's minor philosophical works brought out at Halle, by G. F. Hagent; French translation in J. H. v. Formay's book, *La belle Wolfienne*, ii, published at the Hague; thence the book was again translated into German, as it was very widely read.

[32] Söderblom, *Das Werden des Gottesglaubens*, Leipzig, 1916, quotes, p. 342: " *Cas de conscience sur la commission établie pour réformer des corps réguliers.*" The copy in the *Bibliothèque Nationale* has the pencilled inscription, " *Par D. Clemencet, suivant Bachaumont ou par un dominicain de la rue du Bac.*" 1767.

[33] l.c., p. 343.

[34] Noël, 6 *libri classici sinensis, etc.*, Prag, 1711. To the books already translated in 1687 in *Confucius Sinarum Philosophus* (*Tahsüeh, Chung-Yung, Lun-Yü*), he added the translation of Menzius (*Meng-tzŭ*), *Filialis observantia* (*Hiao-King*) and *Schola Parvulorum* (*San-tzu-Ching*).

[35] *Oratio de Sinarum Philosophia practica*, ed. 1726, p. 65.

[36] l.c., p. 66.

[37] All, *i.e.*, " the children not only of the emperors and kings and famous men, but also of the commonest people."

[38] Wolff, *Oratio de sinarum etc.*, p. 69.

[39] l.c., p. 72.

[40] Frankfurt a. M., 1724.

[41] *Mémoires de l'Académie de Dijon*, 1874, p. 207.

[42] Noël, l.c.

[43] Here it may be further observed that, even in 1662, the principle which guided Intorcetta in his *Sapientia Sinica* was, to judge from his preface, not that of declaring Chinese truth to Europeans, but of providing weapons for the pupils of the mission.

[44] *Lettres édifiantes et curieuses, Recueil* xix, Paris, 1729, p. 483.

[45] *Lettres sur la Morale de Confucius, Philosophe de la Chine*, 1680; and *La Morale de Confucius, Philosophe de la Chine*, 1688.

[46] Voltaire, *Œuvres complètes*, Gotha, 1785, xvi, 85.

[47] *Essai sur les Mœurs*, chap. cxliii.

[48] Voltaire, l.c., xvi, 86.

[49] xxxviii, 482.

[50] xxxviii, 492.

[51] xxxviii, 96.

[52] xxxviii, 492 ff.

[53] xxxviii, 493.

[54] xvi, 272.

[55] xxxi, 410 and xxxviii, 488 ff.

[56] xxxvii, 123.

[57] We find China most fully treated in *Essai sur les Mœurs, Dictionnaire Philosophique*, and in the *Papiers de Jean Nesliers* (Papers of a country-parson), which he edited and which inveigh against the pomp of the Catholic Church and in favour of the simplicity of Abraham, Noah, the Ancients, and China. Also to be noticed is *Du Bannissement des Jésuites*, where he defends the Chinese against the Jesuits.

[58] Voltaire's *Orphelin de la Chine*, published by Leo Jordan, Dresden, 1913, *Gesellschaft für romanische Literatur*, Band 33, Beleg 40, p. 202.

[59] Cheng-Chi-Tong, *Le Théâtre des Chinois*, Paris, 1886, p. 100. Cheng-Chi-Tong is, however, of opinion that Prémare's translation of the drama is a bad one.

[60] Jordan, l.c., p. 90 ff., gives Jordan's exhaustive researches, from which our statements are taken.

[61] l.c., p. 96. Further details about the play and its sources and its history.

[62] *Discours III*, cap. xxix; *Discours IV*, caps. xiii and xiv.

[63] *Voyages d'un Philosophe*, 1769, p. 148 ff.

[64] *Œuvres de Frédéric le Grand*, Berlin, 1853, xxiii, p. 176.

[65] l.c., p. 176.

[66] l.c., xiii, p. 36 ff.

[67] Stimulated by the example of the other powers, Frederick had made an attempt to establish trade-relations with China, but without much success.

[68] *Frédéric le Grand*, l.c., xxiii, p. 365 ff.

[69] l.c., p. 372, and the letter of December 26, 1776, xxiii, p. 39.

[70] l.c., p. 377.

[71] Söderblom, l.c., p. 355.

[72] " Our missionaries represent to us the wide Empire of China as a marvellous state embodying in itself Fear, Honour, and Virtue—I know not what sort of Honour that is, which is attributed to peoples of whom nothing can be made except by floggings."

[73] Montesquieu, *De l'Esprit des Lois*, ed. 1764, Amsterdam-Leipzig, p. 175.

[74] l.c., i, p. 375.

[75] l.c., ii, p. 174.

[76] l.c., ii, p. 175.

[77] l.c., ii, p. 230.

[78] Grimm, *Correspondance littéraire*, September 15, 1766.

[79] *ibid.*, September, 1773.

[80] l.c.

[81] l.c., September, 1776, and February, 1783.

[82] Léon Boulvé, *De l'hellénisme chez Fénelon*, Paris, 1897-8.

[83] Fénelon, *Œuvres choisies*, Paris, 1899, ii, 12-19.

THE PHYSIOCRATS.

[1] Fr. Wolters, *Studien uber Agrarzustände und Agrarprobleme in Frankreich*, 1700–1790, Leipzig, 1905, p. 52.

[2] Morelly, *Code de la Nature*, ed. 1760, and *Les Isles Hottantes ou la Basiliade*, 1753.

[3] Hasbach (*Die allgemeinen philosophischen Grundlagen der von F. Quesnay und Adam Smith begründeten politischen Oekonomie*, Leipzig, 1890) also remarks that Quesnay carefully suppresses his sources, in order to guard his originality. Only so can the uncritical panegyrics of his pupils be explained, p. 149; p. 149 n. " Haller rightly animadverts on the fact that Quesnay never names his authority. Quesnay's theories of blood-letting, of fever, of the healing power of Nature, are moreover not original; they are found in the writings of much more distinguished physicians, who lived before his time or were his contemporaries, for example, Sydenham, Boerhowe, Stahl, as Wunderlich's *History of Medicine* shows." We shall see that at a later time Quesnay in his *Despotisme de la Chine* does acknowledge indebtedness.

[4] F. Quesnay, *Œuvres Économiques et Philosophiques*, ed. A. Oncken, Frankfurt-Paris, 1888, p. 9.

[5] Hasbach, l.c.

[6] Quesnay, l.c., p. 591.

[7] l.c., p. 518 ff.

[8] l.c., p. 375.

[9] l.c., p. 640.

[10] l.c., p. 375.

[11] *Grande Encyclopédie*, éd. 1780, iii, p. 346.
Bülffinger's book treats of the following subjects: (1) The new task of the Philosophy of History (application of philosophy to the state). (2) Chinese moral and political philosophy. (3) The education of the intelligence: how far it can be instructed in the knowledge of Good and Evil. (4) The education of the Will through enthusiasm for Virtue and aversion for Sin. (5) The nature of Passion; its control and use. (6) External action and social converse. (7) The duties and government of the family, ceremonies of mourning, ritual, honouring of parents. (8) The duties of authorities and of princes. (9) The administration of the whole empire. (10) Epilogue: comparison between Chinese wisdom and our philosophy, theology, and morality. The work concludes with a short essay on Chinese literature.

[12] Quesnay, l.c., p. 178.

[13] l.c., p. 376.

[14] l.c., p. 598.

[15] l.c., p. 636.

[16] l.c., p. 636.

[17] l.c., p. 610. I would again point out that Quesnay—like Voltaire —was certainly acquainted with the laws of Jenghiz Khan.

[18] l.c., p. 653.

[19] Baudeau in his *Avertissement du Gouvernement des Incas de Pérou*, 1767; Quesnay, l.c., p. 557.

[20] Eugène Daire, *Physiocrates*, Paris, 1846, i, 798.

THE AGE OF FEELING.

[1] *Nouvelle Héloise, Œuvres de Rousseau*, éd. Paris, 1819, vii, p. 139.

[2] l.c., p. 138 ff.

[3] Shaftesbury, *The Moralists*, 1709, part iii, sec. 2, p. 326.

[4] In the *Spectator* of June 25th, 1712. A hundred years earlier Bacon would have the garden divided into three parts: (1) Greensward with pleached alleys, (2) cultivated garden with a pleasure-house, (3) wilderness.

[5] Th. Whately, *Observations on Modern Gardening*, first ed. 1770, anon., Introduction, p. 1.

[6] Thomas Gray, *Poems and Letters*, ed. Mason, 1820, p. 384.

[7] Louis Le Comte, *Nouveaux mémoires sur l'état présent de la Chine*, Paris, 1696-7, i, p. 336.

[8] E. Kämpfer, *Histoire naturelle, civile et ecclésiastique de l'empire du Japon*, trad. 1729. The Hague, i, chap. iv.

[9] Du Halde, *Description géographique, historique, etc., de l'empire de la Chine et de la Tartarie chinoise*, Paris, 1735, ii, p. 85.

[10] *Lettres édifiantes et curieuses écrites des Missions étrangères*, xxvii, published Paris, 1749. In the ed. of 1781: xxii, p. 1.

[11] *Lettres d'une Société aux Remarques sur quelques ouvrages nouveaux*, Berlin, 1751, i, p. 61.

[12] Voltaire, l.c., x, p. 558.

[13] Whately, *L'Art de former les jardins modernes ou l'art des jardins anglais*, translated into French by Latapie, Paris, 1771.

[14] F. Schiller, *Kleine Schriften vermischten Inhalts*, on the Garden-Calendar for the year 1795.

[15] Lezay-Marnezia, *Essai sur la nature champêtre*, Paris, 1787, p. 155.

[16] W. Chambers, *Essay on Oriental Gardening*, London, 1772; German translation, 1775.

[17] Hirschfeld, *Theorie der Gartenkunst*, 1779, i, p. 127.

[18] W. Chambers, *Plans, Elevations, Sections and Perspective Views of the Gardens and Buildings at Kew in Surrey*, London, 1763.

[19] Laske, l.c., p. 97.

[20] Daniel Mornet, *Le Sentiment de la Nature en France de J. J. Rousseau à Bernardin de Saint-Pierre*, Paris, 1907, p. 458.

[21] Thomson, *Les Saisons*, translated from the English into French by Mme. Bontemps, Paris, 1759, p. 240 ff.

[22] Collected works, Lyon, 1762, iii, pp. 59-72.

[23] Diderot, *Œuvres*, Paris, 1875–1877, xix, p. 182.

[24] Collected works, Paris, 1800, *Voyage en Angleterre*, p. 264 ff.

[25] London, 1777, pp. 140-143.

[26] *Souvenirs d'un Voyageur*, Paris, 1788, i, p. 55.

[27] *Promenades d'automne en Angleterre*, second ed., 1791, pp. 132-139.

[28] *Lettres sur la France, l'Angleterre et l'Italie*, Geneva, 1785, pp. 112-118.

[29] On the laying-out of French gardens in this style, see Mornet, l.c., pp. 233-237.

[30] *Essai sur les Jardins*, 1774.

[31] Laske, l.c., p. 104.

[32] See the illustrations in Chambers, l.c.

[33] There are, of course, points of contact between Chinese, Gothic and modern expressionistic style, but one should beware of drawing too bold analogies. A warning example is an article in *Die Kunst*, October to November, 1920, on 'Rococo and Chinoiserie.'

[34] Quoted by Schumann, l.c., p. 86.

[35] *Histoire de la langue et de la littérature française*, Paris, 1898, vi, p. 752.

[36] Ludwig A. Unzer, *Über die chinesischen Gärten*, Lemgo, 1773, p. 38 ff., note.

[37] Laske, l.c., p. 102.

[38] *ibid.*, p. 99.

[39] *Die Bau- und Kunstdenkmäler im Regierungsbezirk Kassel*, Marburg, 1910, iv, Atlas, Plate 174.

[40] For an attempt to explain this name see *Die Bau- und Kunstdenkmäler im Regierungsbezirk Kassel*, vol. w. text, p. 288, n. 9.

[41] l.c., text, p. 362 f.

[42] Unzer, l.c., Lemgo, 1773. We have also a poem of Unzer on a Chinese theme: *Vou-ti bey Tsin-nas Grabe, eine chinesische Nänie;* it appeared in 1772 at the Brunswick *Waisenbuchhandlung* and was later reprinted in the Göttingen *Musenalmanach*.

[43] Unzer, l.c., p. 11.

[44] l.c., p. 357.

[45] *ibid.*, p. 42.

[46] *ibid.*, p. 44.

[47] *ibid.*, p. 45 ff.

[48] *ibid.*, p. 57.

[49] *ibid.*, p. 81 ff.

[50] According to the *Theorie der Gartenkunst* of Hirschfeld, Leipzig, 1779–1785, quoted in Schumann, l.c., p. 142.

[51] Hirschfeld, l.c., i, p. 81.

[52] For Hirschfeld's remarks on Chinese gardens, see *Gothaer Magazin*, i, 3.

[53] *Le Jardin Anglo-Chinois*, 1770–1787.

[54] Water-colour must not be confused with Tempera. The latter had been long in use, but was always prepared with white-of-egg or lime, partly in order to make it more permanent, partly to give it something of the brilliancy of oil-colour.

[55] *Dict. Univ.*, l.c., iii, p. 898. "Chinese ink is made up in small cakes or sticks, which are dissolved with water on a piece of stoneware or well mixed on an ivory tablet, and then allowed to dry. When it is desired to use it, it is taken up with the brush like other colours."

[56] For further discussion of this question see H. Haas, *Das Spruchgut Kungtses und Laotses in gedanklicher Zusammenordnung*, Leipzig, 1920, especially p. 216 ff. Legge refers to it in his own translation of Lao Tzŭ, p. 115.

[57] The first complete translation of the *Tao Tē Ching* came from Stanislaus Julien, Paris, 1842.

GOETHE.

[1] Woldemar Freiherr von Biedermann, *Goethe-Forschungen*, 3 vols., Frankfurt a. M., 1879, Leipzig, 1886, Leipzig, 1899.

[2] Friedrich Zarncke, *Kleine Schriften*, Bd. i, *Goethe-Schriften*, Leipzig, 1897.

[3] *Goethes sämtliche Werke*, Stuttgart-Berlin, 1902-1912 (Cotta), ' Jubiläums-Ausgabe '), xxiii, p. 170.

[4] l.c., xxii, p. 120.

[5] ' Jubiläums-Ausgabe,' l.c., xxii, p. 183.

[6] *ibid.*, xxxvi, p. 38.

[7] *ibid.*, vii, p. 251.

[8] *Goethes gesammelte Werke*, Weimar, 1887 ff., xxxvii, p. 311.

[9] Biedermann, l.c., iii, p. 196.

[10] Riemer, *Mitteilungen uber Goethe*, Berlin, 1841, ii, p. 825.

[11] Biedermann, l.c., i, pp. 94-123; ii, pp. 132-159; Fr. Zarncke, *Kleine Schriften*, Leipzig, 1897, Bd. i; Georg Ellinger, l.c., p. 262 ff.

[12] *Briefwechsel zwischen Goethe und Schiller*, 3 Bde., Leipzig, 1912, ii, p. 103.

[13] ' Jubiläums-Ausgabe,' xxx, p. 126.

[14] *ibid.*, ix, p. 9.

[15] *Briefwechsel*, l.c., i, p. 224.

[16] *ibid.*, i, p. 225.

[17] ' Jubiläums-Ausgabe,' xiii, p. 292.

[18] *ibid.*, ix, p. 339.

[19] Weimar ed., xl, p. 83-84.

[20] ' Jubiläums-Ausgabe,' xxx, p. 275-276.

[21] *ibid.*, xxxvii, p. 222.

[22] *ibid.*, xxx, p. 407.

[23] *ibid.*, xxxv, p. 158.

[24] *ibid.*, xxxvii, p. 210. The reference is again to *Lao-sheng-ērhl* of 1817, a play which had appeared that year in London, and had been translated into German by Moritz Engelhardt in the *Morgenblatt* (April 10 to 22, 1818).

[25] Weimar ed., xxiv, p. 152.

[26] ' Jubiläums-Ausgabe,' xxxviii, p. 153.

[27] Weimar ed., xlix, p. 51 f.

[28] ' Jubiläums-Ausgabe,' xxxviii, p. 278.

[29] Verses 6856–6864 of the Second Part.

[30] Biedermann, l.c., ii, pp. 426-445.

[31] Weimar ed., v, pp. 50-51.

[32] ' Jubiläums-Ausgabe,' xxxviii, pp. 101 ff.

[33] The reference is to the novel, *Yü Chiao Li*, which Rémusat had translated into French in 1826 under the title *Les deux cousines*, and which appeared in a German form as *Die beiden Basen*, in 1827.

[34] He refers to the ten Chinese *Novellen*, which Rémusat translated into French in 1827, and which were thence translated into German in the same year; Rémusat had taken them from the English of Davis: *Chinese Novels* (1822).

[35] Weimar ed., xlix, p. 214.

LAST WORDS.

[1] De Guignes, *Examen critique des Annales chinoises ou Mémoire sur l'incertitude des douze premiers siècles de ces Annales, et de la chronologie chinoise.—Rec. de l'Académie, Mem. xxxvi*, 1774, pp. 164-189; also *Réflexions sur quelques passages rapportés par les Missionaires, concernant la Chronologie chinoise.* Read on January 15th, 1779; *Rec. de l'Academie des Inscr., Mem. xliii*, 1786, pp. 239-286.

[2] Jones, *Discours sur les Chinois*, 1790, in *Recherches Asiatiques*, 1805, p. 401 ff.

[3] *The Chinese Traveller*, collected from Du Halde, Le Comte, and other modern travellers, second ed., London, 1775.

[4] Priscilla Wakefield was the author's name; the book was translated into French: F. M. de Beaumont, *Beautés de l'histoire de la Chine, du Japon et des Tartares . . . Ouvrage consacré à l'instruction de la Jeunesse*, second ed., Paris, 1825.

[5] Söderblom, l.c., p. 357.

[6] Christoph Meiners, *Ubersetzungen der Abhandlungen chinesischer Jesuiten über die Geschichte, Wissenschaften und Künste, Sitten und Gebräuche der Chinesen*, Bd. i, Leipzig, 1778, p. 74.

[7] Meiners, l.c., p. 77.

[8] *ibid.*, l.c., p. 83.

[9] Joseph Hager, *Panthéon Chinois ou parallèle entre le culte religieux des Grecs et celui des Chinois, etc.*, Paris, 1806.

[10] Meiners, l.c., p. 318.

[11] Illustration in Richard Graul, *Das 18. Jahrhundert, Dekoration und Mobiliar* (*Handbücher Preussischer Museen in Berlin*), 1905, p. 169.

[12] In the 1760's, for example, periodicals for coin-collectors sprang up like mushrooms in Germany.

[13] Söderblom, l.c.

INDEX

Absolutism, 35, 88, 94, 101
Addison, Joseph, 114, 115
Agriculture, 106
Amphitrite, the, 34, 40
Anson, *Voyages:* 95n., 96, 138
Architecture, Chinese influence, 55, 57–8, 60–6, 119–20, 132
— gardens, 65, 66, 118–20, 122
— Rococo, 55–6
— roofs, 63–4
— windows, 61, 70
Argens, Marquis d', 69
Art, Laoism and, 8

Baudeau, Abbé, 105, 109
Bauer, Ferdinand, 140
Bayle, Pierre, 25
Bérain, Jules, 51, 53, 70
Bossuet and China, 79–80, 90
Böttger, 28
Boucher, F., 45, 50, 53
Boucher, J. F., 152
Briseux, 55
Bruhl, palace, 63
Bülffinger, 87

Caffieri, 30
Chaises, 35–6
Chambers, 66, 119, 121,125
— *Essay on Oriental Gardening*, 116–18
Chauveau, J., 46
Chien-iung, 54, 92
China, notions of, 18ff., 88
— as market, 150
Chinese culture, origins, 151

Chinese Pleasure Garden, 20n.
Chinoiseries, 32, 50, 52, 62, 137 –8, 141
Christall, J., 125
Chung-yung, 20
Classical revival, 130, 135, 142, 151, 152
Colbert, 18, 102
Cologne, Archbishop of, 36, 63
Colour, 43, 152
Condorcet, schools, 87, 108n.
Confucius, critics of, 98
— and Enlightenment, 149
— and Lao-Tzu, 7, 76
— on morality, 84
— and natural order, 52, 104
— and state structure, 77
— translations, 20, 77, 88, 138

de Bodt, Jean, 60
Decker, P., 54
Descartes, rejection, 113
de Pastoret: *Zoroastre, Confuzius et Mahomet*, 78
Despotism, enlightened, 88, 96, 106
Diderot: *Encyclopédie*, 92, 106
Drawing, 49, 50, 140
Dresden, Japanese palace, 60
du Halde, Marquis, 78, 115, 135
Dutch adaptations, Chinese art, 47, 80

East India Companies, 16, 17, 18, 21, 37, 38, 39, 40

Education, 70, 86, 107–8
Embassies, 19, 139
Embroidery, 44–5
England, Chinese influence, 26, 45, 114ff., 125
— relations with China, 150–1
— Rococo in, 71, 72
Engraving, 19, 52
Enlightenment, the, 11, 75ff., 126, 149
— and Rococo, 113
Erhardt, G. and F., 46
Essarts, 70
Eucken, R., 3

Faience, 28, 29
Fans, 50n.
Fénelon, 96–7, 98
Fireworks, 67
Flower-Paper, 144–5
France, art, Chinese influence, 28, 34, 53, 54
— Chinese fashions, 38, 50, 59, 70
— Chinese studies, 85, 92, 103
— Eastern trade, 18
— silk manufacture, 42–3
Franciscus, Erasmus, 20n.
Franck, Otto, 5
Francke, A. H., 83–4
Frederick the Great, 31, 34–5, 57n., 61, 69
— and Chinese philosophy, 84
— and gardens, 121
— and Rousseau, 94
— and Voltaire, 34–5, 92, 93
Furniture, 27, 64, 70, 71

Gardens, as art, 115
— Chinese style, 62, 66, 114ff., 120, 123–5
— English, 119, 122, 125

formal, 114, 116, 125
— Goethe on, 132–3
— landscape, 125
— natural, 112, 125
— philosophy of, 122
— and sentiment, 122–3, 149
Gillot, flower paintings, 52
Gobelins tapestries, 45
Goethe, 129–46
— *Chinaman in Rome*, 137
— Chinese studies, 131, 139, 140, 143
— *Chinesedeutsche Zeiten*, 129, 139, 143, 145
— chinoiserries, 137–8, 141–2
— and classical art, 130, 142
— early views on China, 129, 130
— *Elpenor*, 129, 133, 135, 139
— *Faust*, 143
— on gardens, 132–3
— on philosophy, 131, 138, 146
— on theatre, 133–5, 141
— Triumph of Sentiment, 120, 131–2
Gold, 17–18
Goldfish, 67
Gotskowski, 31n.
Gothic and Chinese architecture, 65–6, 119–20, 146
Grimm: *Correspondence litteraire*, 92n.
Grudar: *Espion Chinois*, 69
Hager, J., 151
Halfpenny: *Sheleters, Porticoes and Pavilions*, 120
Helvetius, 92
Herder, 131, 135
Herold, 29, 54
Hirschfeld on gardens, 118, 123–4

Holland, Chinese imports, 19, 26, 60, 61
— gardens, 125
Huguier, J. G., 46, 53, 54
Hult, Christoph, 52

Indian mysticism, 153
Italy, 42, 68

Jablonski, 81
Japan, 30, 36, 115
Jeaurat, 50
Jesuits, decline of influence, 149, 150
— and Confucius, 20, 85
— reports of China, 18, 20, 32, 54, 56, 58, 82, 94, 102, 105, 115
— Voltaire and, 78

Kämpfer: *History of Japan*, 115
Kassel, Chinese colony, 121–2
Kew Gardens, 118–9
Kircher, Athanasius, 19, 79
Klaproth, 84, 139
Ko, 102–3
Ku Hung-ming, 3, 10
Kung Fu-Tzu, see *Confucius*
Lacquer, 34, 36–7, 44, 70, 131
Lao-Tzu, 7–11, 26, 52
— and Confucius, 76, 78
— Goethe and, 138
— Tao, 79
Le Comte, Pere, 21, 26, 56, 65, 115
Leibniz, 76, 79–81, 82
— *Ars Combinatoria*, 82
Liversedge, H., 125–6
Louis XIV, 44, 114, 116
— style, 152
Louvois, 39–40

Magdeborg Cathedral, 140
Majolica, 27
Martin, Robert, 34

Martini, Martino, 19, 65, 139
Marot, Daniel, 44
Masques, 149
Mathematics, 82, 83, 109
Maupertius, 113
Meiners, Christoph, 151
Meissen, 27, 28–9, 31
Meissonier, 52, 56, 57
Mercure galant, 38
Middle class, rise of, 152–3
Mirabeau, Marquis de, 34, 103–4
Mirror painting, 30–2
Missionaries, see *Jesuits*
Monbijou palace, 32
Montesquieu, 69, 91, 94, 95
Morality, public, 7, 87, 89, 146
Morelly, 101–2
Muller: *Clavis Sinica*, 19, 79–80

Namur, Duchesse de, 35
Nanking, porcelain tower, 66
Natural law, 88, 101–2, 106
Nature, return to, 6–7, 48, 113ff.
— Rococo, 47n, 48, 76
Noël, Père, 86–8, 131
Novus Atlas Sinensis, 19
Nymphenburg, 60, 63

Opera, 68–9

Pagodas, 59–61, 65, 66
— European, 118–122
Painting, 47–9, 52, 125–6
Pannwitz, Rudolf, 9, 10
Papillon, Jean, 46
Pascal, 20
Pauw, 93, 139, 142
Pavilions, 57, 61, 63
Peking, 59, 66, 115
Petersburg, Smolny monastery, 65
Pétis de la Croix, 107, 108
Peyrotte, 53, 54
Physiocrats, 86–7, 101–9, 149

Pillement, J., 44, 52, 53, 54
Poetry, 93, 141
Poivre: *Ravels of a Philosopher*, 92
Politics and morality, 87
Polo, Marco, 15, 16, 139
Pompadour, Mme. de, 34, 67, 102, 106
Pope, Alexander, 114, 115
Poppelmann, 60
Porcelain, 18, 26, 27–30
— Arita, 26, 30
— European manufacture, 28, 29–34
— examples, 27, 30ff., 60n., 152
— Meissen, 27–31
— Nanking tower, 60n., 66
— and Rococo, 37
Portuguese discoveries, 15–16, 29, 50
Potsdam, 61, 62
Prémare, 91, 133–5
Prints, books, 53–4

Quesnay and China, 76, 101–2, 104–6
— *Le Despotisme de la Chine*, 104, 106, 108
— *Tableau economique*, 109

Remusat, 126
Religion, 9, 78–9, 95–6, 136
Rococo, 25ff.
— Chinese affinities, 25–6, 149
— English, 71, 72
— and Enlightenment, 75ff., 113
— France, 42
— relations with China, 128
— social life, 71
— style, 25, 43, 49, 152
Rogg, G., 54
Rousseau, 91, 94, 95n., 114, 120

— and Lao-Tzu, 7, 8, 120
Rückert: *Oestliche Rosen*, 140

Sapientia Sinica, 20
Sans Souci palace, 62–3
Schadow, Gottfried, 152
Schiller, 116, 132, 135–6
— *Turandot*, 138, 141
Sculpture, 54n.
Silk imports, 17, 37, 38
— European manufacture, 39–43, 46, 83, 121
— smuggling, 41–2
Silver, 17–18, 33
Sinologists, 84
Social life, 66, 67, 71
Spicelius, 79
State and morality, 77, 87, 89
Stern, Chinese buildings, 61
Stobwasser, 36, 37
Sung dynasty, 26, 48
Switzerland, 61
Symmetry, 25, 52

Tapestry, 53
Taxation, 108–9
Tea, 17, 19, 27
Textiles, 40–4, 46
Theatre, 66–7, 68–9, 141
Theism, 89, 114
Tolstoi, 5, 7, 8
Trianon de Pourcelaine, 60
Turgot, school plans, 87, 108n.

Unzen, L. A.: *On Chinese Gardens*, 122

Venice, 27
Versailles, 51, 70
Virtue, idea, 79, 85, 89, 93
— Quesnay on, 105, 107
— teaching of, 86
Voltaire on China, 69, 78–9, 142
— on Confucius, 89–90

— enlightened despotism, 106

— *Essai sur les moeurs*, 79, 90, 91, 95

— and Frederick the Great, 34–5, 92, 93

— on gardens, 115

— *L'Homme aux quarante écus*, 109

— on Jesuits, 78, 87, 88

— *Orphelin de la Chine*, 89, 90–1

— on Rousseau, 91

von Humboldt, 84, 126
von Schirnau, 28n.

Wallpaper, 45–7
Watteau, 47, 48–50
Weaving, 41–3
Whateley, Thos. 115, 119
Wolff, Christian, 83, 84, 86, 87

Zen, 26
Zend-Avesta, 78n.
Zoroaster, 78n.

Figure 1. Kang-hsi Vase

Figure 2. Eighteenth-century teapot with Chinese figures

Figure 3. Eighteenth-century lacquered French commode

Figure 4. Chinese woven silk tapestry

Figure 5. Chinese painting on silk

Figure 6. Chinese fan, painted, with lacquered spokes

Figure 7. Chinoiserie of Watteau

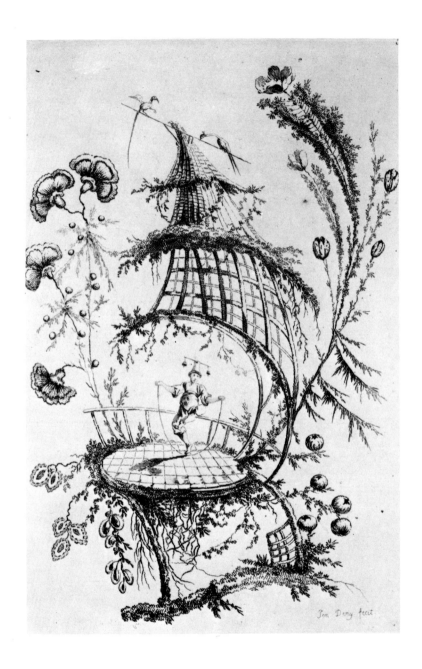

Figure 8. From Pillement's series of prints

Figure 9. French engraving of Chinese battle scene

Figure 10. French engraving of Chinese battle scene

Figure 11. Munich, the Queen's salon

Figure 12. The 'Japanischer Pavillon' at Sans-Souci

Figure 13. The Chinese influence on furniture

Figure 14. Imitation of Lattice Work

Figure 15. French commode, eighteenth century.

Figure 16. Sowing rice

Figure 17. Chinese rice farmers

Figure 18. Doorway at Claydon House

Figure 19. 'Chinese' bedroom at Claydon House

Figure 20. Pagoda in Shanghai

Figure 21. Pagoda in Kew Gardens

Figure 24. Po Yo Bridge

Figure 25. The garden at Stourhead, Wilts

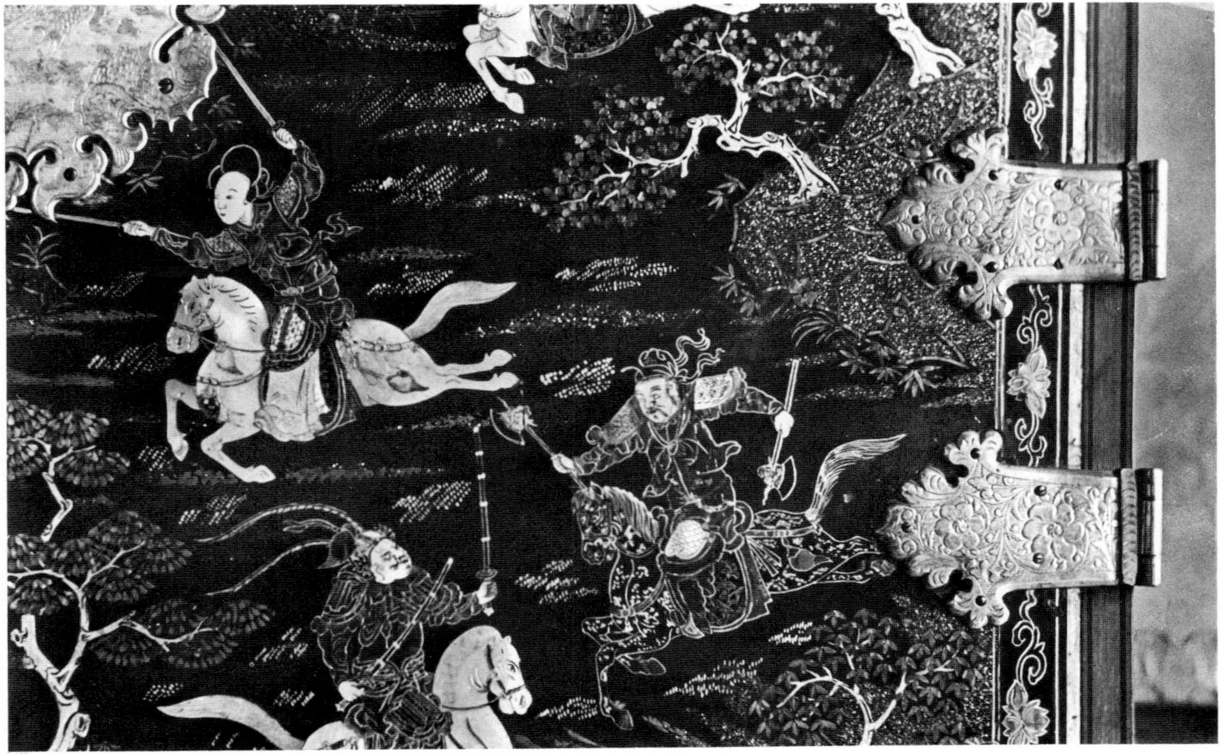

Figure 26. Lacquered cabinet at Charlottenburg